REFUGEES WORLDWIDE

Literary Reportage

COMPILED BY LUISA DONNERBERG
AND ULRICH SCHREIBER

 Ragpicker Press

Refugees Worldwide – Literary Reportage
First published by Ragpicker Press Ltd. in 2017

These pieces have been written, translated and published with the support of:
Auswärtiges Amt
Heinrich-Böll-Stiftung
Konrad-Adenauer-Stiftung
Institut Ramon Llull
Fondation Jan Michalski
Japan Foundation Köln

Royalties from sales of this book will be donated to Refugees International.

ISBN 978-0-9929161-4-5
eBook ISBN 978-0-9929161-5-2

Project coordinator: Lucy Curzon
Text design, typesetting and eBook by Tetragon, London
Copy-edited by Jethro Soutar, Lucy Curzon and Rachael McGill
Proofread by Sarah Terry
Cover design by Finn Dean
Cover art by Rubab Paracha. From her Flowing Borders project:
Germany – Pakistan. High density areas for refugees and migrants in Pakistan and Germany.

Printed and bound by T.J. International, Padstow, Cornwall

CONTENTS

FOREWORD

*My sister, whom I haven't seen for more than two years, told
me she was going to cross the sea in a rubber dinghy. Then she
hung up. She didn't want to hear what I thought…*

KHALED KHALIFA

This is a book about one of the greatest challenges of our age.
We present fourteen literary accounts of migration: its causes;
its impact on identity; its repercussions when deemed successful
and when a failure. Behind the statistics lie diverse stories of
displacement, exile and the reasons why people leave everything behind. In this collection, fourteen authors from thirteen
countries and four continents reflect on different aspects of the
refugee experience. To help them in their understanding, some
travelled by plane or by car, others on foot, mostly within their
own countries, to focal points on the refugee trail. Others travelled inwards, to navigate emotional worlds. They share their
discoveries in these thought-provoking texts. The Peter Weiss
Foundation for Art and Politics, which initiated and managed
the 'Refugees Worldwide' project, was eager for authors to
explore the theme. Literature is uniquely placed to express the
quirks of individual fate.

According to the Global Trends Report produced by the
United Nations High Commissioner for Refugees (UNHCR),
there were 65 million forcibly displaced people in the world in
2015. There has been no reduction in global instability since
then. Civil war still rages in Syria, Ukraine remains precarious.

The biggest refugee camp in the world, Dadaab in Kenya, houses over 400,000 people, spanning several generations. As long as crises continue, people will continue to flee towards Europe.

However, most of the stories in this book do not take place in Europe. We wanted to challenge the Eurocentric approach that dominates European media. Instead, we allow Masatsugu Ono to tell us about the life of a Congolese refugee in Tokyo, and we begin to see how widely attitudes to refugees differ across the world. According to official statistics, Japan took in a total of twenty-eight refugees in 2015. In Nigeria, huge numbers of internally displaced people flee terrorist organisations like Boko Haram, which control the North East of the country. We hope this book will contribute to an increased awareness that this is not primarily a European problem, and help broaden perspectives and deepen our thinking about refugees.

LUISA DONNERBERG AND
ULRICH SCHREIBER, JUNE 2017

EXILE IS MY IDENTITY

NORA BOSSONG

Translated from the German by Kurt Beals

NORA BOSSONG was born in Bremen in 1982 and studied Philosophy and Comparative Literature in Berlin, Leipzig and Rome. She is the author of several successful novels and poetry collections including *Webers Protokoll* [Weber's Protocol] (2009), *36,9°* (2015), *Rotlicht* [Red Light] (2017) and *Sommer vor den Mauern* [Summer in front of the Walls] (2011), for which she received the 2012 Peter Huchel Prize. She has also received several other awards including the Berlin Art Prize (2011) and the Roswitha Prize (2016).

KURT BEALS is Assistant Professor in the Department of Germanic Languages and Literatures at Washington University in St. Louis. His research focuses on German experimental poetry in a media-historical context. He has translated a number of German works into English, including books by Anja Utler, Regina Ullmann and Reiner Stach, and has received awards and honours including the German Book Office Translation Prize and a PEN/Heim Translation Fund Grant.

'THERE are no truths, just forms to fill in.' This phrase would stick in my head for a long time after I heard it from people in New York who'd come to America seeking asylum. I'd come seeking insight: to find out what 'homeland' meant to these people and to gain a better understanding of the situation in the United States, a nation of immigrants, and in New York, a city open to the world, in a year when the presidential election looked like it might be won by a Republican candidate calling for a high wall along the Mexican border and a ban on immigration for Muslims.

It's late summer, 2016, and I'm in New York for two weeks to get an impression of the conditions faced by people who come here as refugees or asylum seekers. New York City is widely considered to be an especially liberal and multicultural metropolis, and New York State is supposedly among the three US states with the largest refugee populations, although after a few days I sense that none of them live in the metropolitan region any more. 'The refugees in our assistance programme have been resettled,' one aid agency tells me. New York City is just too expensive. Henrike, from the organisation IRAP (International Refugee Assistance Project), dryly notes that the US authorities have a hard time even meeting the quota of 10,000 Syrian refugees who are supposed to be accepted each year for resettlement across the entire country, which is only a fifth of the number that Canada plans to accept in the same period. But so far not even half that many have arrived in the US. And a friend tells me he knows some undocumented immigrants, but they're afraid of getting into trouble with the authorities. They certainly wouldn't want to talk to a reporter.

It sounds almost luxurious when I hear that the young man and the two families I'm finally able to meet arrived in America by plane holding tourist visas; that they didn't have to sneak across the Mexican border like the men I met in the waiting room of Central American Legal Assistance (CALA), who fled Ciudad Juaréz for Texas without papers, under the cover of darkness, relying on luck alone to help them evade the Border Patrol. Housed in a run-down basement in the west of Brooklyn, with a map of Central America hanging on the wall, the NGO offers free legal assistance to asylum seekers from all countries between Mexico and Colombia.

'But we can't even begin to advise them all,' says Heather, one of the lawyers who works here. 'There are just too many people who don't have any chance of success, in our view.' It's often better if they don't even try, she tells me, because anyone whose asylum application is rejected will immediately be sent back. Instead, they usually stay in the country as 'unauthorised immigrants', whose numbers are currently estimated at roughly eleven million, most of them from Mexico. It's a status that's hard to imagine for those of us who come from a welfare state context like Germany. On the one hand, the authorities aren't officially supposed to know about them and they're not allowed to receive any public support or be given a legal work permit; on the other hand, their children are allowed to attend school and they have the right to some essential healthcare and even a City ID card, available to all New York City residents. And it's always possible to find work off the books, on a small or a large scale. Even Donald Trump was happy to make use of these low-cost workers, as Hillary Clinton pointed out in one of the presidential debates.

Some of the new arrivals have been caught and sent back before, Heather says, but they try again anyway. I can't help but think of Sisyphus, except the stones that roll down the mountain over and over again are the people themselves. At the end of our conversation, I ask Heather if the situation will get worse if Trump wins the election. 'Trump isn't going to win,' she answers categorically, and adds somewhat more softly, 'That would be a disaster.'

Venezuela was actually never a land of emigration, Wendy tells me as she gives me a glass of water. Everyone wanted to stay. She was an exception, she came here twenty-six years ago to study, met the man who's now her husband, and stayed. Luisa is several years younger than Wendy. She studied international relations at the Universidad Central de Venezuela and then went to Ecuador, where she worked at the Venezuelan embassy. She was responsible for Venezuelans imprisoned there, people who had spent years in jail without their families even knowing what had happened to them. The ambassador already had a permanent position in mind for Luisa, but then he asked her if she'd voted for Chávez in the last election. No, she said, she didn't agree with Chávez's politics. It was after that conversation that the problems started.

The permanent position was never mentioned again and a month later Luisa had to go back to Venezuela. She looked for jobs in Caracas, but found closed doors wherever she turned. When Luisa's daughter came down with a middle-ear infection and she couldn't get hold of any antibiotics – the pharmacies were empty, the doctors just shrugged – it became clear to her that she had to leave the country. 'What's going on in Venezuela right now,' Freddy angrily interjects, 'is a violation of human rights. There are food shortages in the grocery stores, and it's getting more and more dangerous on the streets.' Freddy is sitting off to the side in an armchair, carefully following the conversation. Like Luisa, he only came to the United States a few months ago.

Luisa tells me that she tried living in Mexico, but she couldn't keep her head above water there. Six months ago, she arrived in Orlando, found a room for herself and her daughter, and even had a lead on a job. 'But she would have been paid by cheque,' Wendy says, 'and she can't cash them if she only has a tourist visa. And if she left her daughter at home alone while she went to work, she'd get in trouble with the authorities. I told her to go to a lawyer for advice.' In June, Luisa came to New York with her daughter; next week she'll be fingerprinted, then her residency status will change from tourist to asylum seeker. She thinks she has a chance of success.

'The situation in Venezuela isn't going to change any time soon,' says Freddy, 'it's the Wild West down there.' He tells me about one of the last Sundays he spent there. Around mid-morning, two armed men broke into his house. Freddy crept into his bedroom and loaded his pistol. And then fired. That was the moment he decided to leave Venezuela.

I'm waiting for Alex in a café in Manhattan's Financial District. While I sip my iced tea and look at the young people at the tables around me, I wonder whether anyone in New York actually sympathises with Trump, whether his campaign slogan, 'Make America Great Again', has any appeal here. New York isn't a Republican stronghold, but Trump did win the primaries here and this city is his home. So far I've heard nothing but negative things about him. Yesterday, for instance, I visited a man named Don in his office at a think tank for migration policy. 'Trump would ruin America,' he said, adding that people on Wall Street were already betting on a Trump victory and investors were beginning to pull their money out of the country. When I stopped by a neighbour's place for a glass of wine one evening, his predictions were no less bleak. 'Then it'll be just like Venezuela here,' he said. But he agreed that Trump couldn't possibly win. Am I just living in a bubble, where I only meet people who largely share my political views?

Alex stands in front of me, laughing and a bit nervous. He grew up in the Russian city of Togliatti, where he says there wasn't much besides car factories. The Detroit of the East, I think. He came to the United States on a work and travel programme, now he's studying, continuing to perfect his excellent English, working and earning money. He's clearly proud of his work ethic. He already feels more like an American than a Russian, and he's thinking of changing his last name so that he doesn't sound so Slavic. I think of a passage from Vladimir Nabokov about the absurd attempts of some Americans to correctly pronounce the Russian name Pnin. But it's not just a matter of pronunciation for Alex. Ideally he'd like to take the name of his grandmother-in-law, 'a good German name', even if he can't remember it right now.

He tells me that he'll get his green card soon. The asylum process hasn't been hard for him, a friend helped him with the documents and prepared him for the interview, he stayed up late at night getting ready for it. By now he can't even imagine what it would be like to have to live in Russia again, in the oppressive atmosphere of the city where he was born, under a president named Putin. Again and again, Alex emphasises how grateful he is to live in America, and how much he loves the freedom here. The only thing that bothers him is that more and more Asians keep moving into the neighbourhood where he and his husband live. In his first job here in New York he only worked with African Americans, but that was too much for him, so he quit after a few days. Alex dreams of living in a white, middle-class city, where he can be around people like himself.

He asks me what I think about the politics of migration in Europe. Don't I agree that Muslims have no place in Western society? That they're infiltrating our culture? I smile at him uncomprehendingly. I hadn't expected questions like that here, in the middle of the apparently liberal city of New York, from a friendly-looking young man. I respond that some of my best and most European friends are Muslims. But Alex insists that there's a difference between Christian culture and Islam – each one has its place, but there isn't room for both of them in Europe. 'In the end,' he says, 'you'll feel like an immigrant in your own land.'

I try to keep smiling, even as I wonder how someone who has experienced discrimination due to his sexual orientation can judge other people like this, based on their religion, their nationality, the colour of their skin. The desire to be white, to have a German last name, to live in a neighbourhood free of 'others'... Would he even have met me if my name were Nora Morales and I worked for a Mexican newspaper? I don't ask him what he thinks of Donald Trump.

'If you want asylum,' Tsamchoe tells me, 'you can't tell the truth, you have to tell a story, it can be a lie, but it has to sound good. And you have to have the papers to prove it, that's the most important thing.'

We're sitting in her small apartment deep in Queens, near Corona Park, where her four children share the two bedrooms. Her oldest daughter, Khachoe, is sitting with us and translating for her mother. The tiny living room is adorned with colourful Tibetan prayer flags, with Tsamchoe's bed and a dressing table in the middle, both decorated with elaborate carvings. She had the furniture sent to her from Tibet, it makes her feel closer to home. And she knows she can never go back, not even for a brief visit.

Still, Tsamchoe hesitantly says, she's happy that she came to America. She has a job as a maid in a hotel, where she works as much as she can in order to provide for her children. She never wanted to depend on government assistance. She's been here for eight years, her youngest children were born in America, and Khachoe has spent most of her life here. Khachoe is twenty years old, she's looking forward to returning to college one day, but she had to withdraw because she didn't have enough money for tuition. I ask her if she feels American after all these years. Or if she feels Tibetan, even though she never experienced Tibet for herself. Khachoe thinks for a while. She tells me that she feels Tibetan, but she's part of a new generation, a generation of Tibetans who were born and raised in exile. 'I can imagine what a lot of things are like there, but I'll never really know what it means to be a Tibetan in Tibet. I'm a Tibetan in exile, that's my identity.'

Tsamchoe met her second husband in America, a Tibetan man with US citizenship. If she hadn't married him, things would be worse for her family, even today. They were never granted asylum. 'So many people in our family were political prisoners. We have books and articles that mention them, but the authorities wouldn't accept them. There are no truths here, there are just forms to fill in.' Tsamchoe's daughter translates for her, then adds, 'That's the American way.' I don't know if this is part of the translation or if she's adding her own commentary to her mother's story.

Back when Tsamchoe came to America with her children and set off on the never-ending path through American government agencies, her father and one of her brothers were imprisoned in Tibet, having been arrested during the Tibetan unrest of the late 1980s. 'The Chinese government wanted to purge everything, to impose a new Chinese identity,' her daughter says. Tsamchoe's father was later killed by the army. Armed soldiers marched right into private rooms, says the mother, intimidating people, demanding they share their belongings. 'That's the communist way,' says the daughter.

Tsamchoe speaks quickly. She says her English isn't good enough, even though we had a conversation without an interpreter just a few days ago. Maybe it's not about her English at all, maybe she just finds it a bit easier to tell this story in her native tongue. Some people, she says, were able to get papers even though they'd never been in jail. Then there were prisoners who'd been tortured, but when they were released they didn't have any papers. After all, who issues certificates for abuse? 'In Tibetan culture we trust people, we don't put much down on paper,' she says. One of the most important lessons she's learned is that it's different here. She still blames herself for not figuring that out before she arrived.

After my visit to Queens, I take the 7 train to Bryant Park in Manhattan to go for a walk. It's another one of those blazing hot days in New York, the sky an almost artificial blue. The cover of *Time* magazine shows Donald Trump melting like a scoop of ice cream. The headline: 'Meltdown'. Is this the last, perhaps all-too naive sign of hope that remains for America's great 'melting pot'?

The traffic in the streets is hardly moving, pedestrians hurry past me. I walk slowly, thinking about the people I've met here. They arrived months or years ago, many of them believing that this was the Promised Land, the great dream of freedom, only to run up against the internal borders of bureaucracy and resentment. They experience these borders when they discover that even here, some people don't want to share their apartment buildings with people of a different religion or skin colour; when they comprehend that they'll never be able to travel back to their native countries where the rest of their families live; when they learn that it isn't their histories that count, it isn't their own identities, it's their stamped papers, as if the people these papers represent didn't even exist.

PERMANENT TRANSIT

ARTEM CHAPEYE

Translated from the Russian by Marian Schwartz

ARTEM CHAPEYE was born in Ukraine in 1981 and has worked as a publisher for a children's magazine, as a translator and as a reporter for the Ukrainian foreign ministry. His debut novel *Awantjura* [An Adventure] (2008), was followed by *Podorosh iz Mamajotoju v poschukach Ukraini* [Travels with Mamayota: In Search of Ukraine] (2011) and *Tscherwona zona* [The Red Zone] (2014). His collection of reportage *Wojna na tri bukwy* [War in Three Letters] (2015), was nominated for the International Kurt Schork Journalism Award.

MARIAN SCHWARTZ has translated Russian fiction, history, criticism and fine arts for over forty years, including such classics as *Oblomov*, *A Hero of Our Time* and *Anna Karenina*. Her translation of Leonid Yuzefovich's *Harlequin's Costume* won the 2014 Read Russia Prize. She lives in Austin, Texas.

'I don't look like a *bomzh*?' He eyed me warily. 'Really?'

Bomzh is pretty harsh – not just homeless, more like a tramp – but right now that's exactly what he is. Homeless, here in Kharkiv.

We're at the bus depot. Smoking. He's showing me his ID, his own and his son's. The ten-year-old is sitting up against the wall on his black gym bag. Where the child's mother is I don't know, and I don't feel comfortable asking. Their papers say that the man and boy are from Alchevsk. Alchevsk is currently under the control of the 'Luhansk People's Republic' (LPR or LNR).

'If we don't get on the bus today, I don't know where we're going to spend the night,' the man says.

We each take a drag.

No, he doesn't look like your stereotypical homeless Ukrainian. He looks very working-class. He's between thirty and forty; it's hard to say exactly. Worn but polished black shoes. Black jeans. A light grey jacket. Hair cut short and combed back. He hasn't been to a dentist in a long time; it's amazingly easy to determine a person's social status by their teeth. A tanned face from working all summer in private construction in Kharkiv, hauling wheelbarrows of cement. The dry season ended and so did the work.

The man scarcely differs from anyone else at the depot. Internal refugees who have the official status of internally displaced persons don't differ from other people in any outward way. In Ukraine, there are about a million and a half of them, but those million and a half are virtually invisible. The displaced melt away into the cities, primarily the big cities. A million and a half invisible people. It's not written on their faces that they fled shooting or the poverty that accompanies war. Their exact number can only be estimated. Human rights activists say there are more internal refugees than the official figures report because not everyone is registered. At the same time, the resettlers themselves are saying more and more often that many people they know are going home, although they're still registered in territory under government control.

The man from Alchevsk and his son have spent nearly a year in Kharkiv, but can't go on. His casual earnings aren't enough to rent permanent housing. Right now they're going back to their home town, where at least they still have a home. But they don't even have enough for the tickets.

The father isn't asking for money. He takes out a couple of bank notes to show me, two hundred apiece. But this little isn't enough. He's asking me to buy them tickets home and will give me everything he has. There's pain in his eyes. He's not used to asking and feels humiliated. Humiliated for himself and for his son, who is watching him closely from his perch on his bag.

When Western reporters came here after the conflict, they started asking local fixers to take them to 'refugee camps'. They probably pictured large fields and tents, like those they'd seen in Turkey or Lebanon for Syrian refugees. But there wasn't anything like that in Ukraine.

The people fleeing the war melted away into the general population. They rented housing in Kramatorsk, Kharkiv, Izium, Kyiv, Dnipro and Zaporizhia. They lived with relatives or acquaintances. At worst, they settled in children's summer camps or uninhabited state premises, where volunteers or the state brought furniture. The resettlers didn't stand out in any way from the locals in either appearance or language. Often they were practically local themselves. Most internal refugees moved within the borders of Donetsk Oblast, some of which is controlled by the government and some by the unrecognised 'Donetsk People's Republic' (DPR or DNR). The second most common destination for reluctant refugees was the nearest metropolis, Russian-speaking Kharkiv.

The first transit village, built with money from the German Society for International Cooperation, opened in Kharkiv in January 2015. The only people the state settles there are single mothers and families with multiple children or disabled dependants.

'Can you tell me where the resettlers' village is?'

'You mean there is one?'

'Yes, somewhere near here.'

'First I've heard.'

'Thanks.'

Spring is late. It's cold outside. There's wet snow on the ground. I've walked by a reinforced concrete factory and an abandoned industrial zone, but there's no resettlers' village anywhere to be seen. It still doesn't even have a precise address.

'Excuse me, do you know where the village for resettlers is?'

'Are you going there? Maybe you need something. We have a couple of blankets.'

...

'I don't think there's any more room in the village, though.'

'Ah! That's what you mean. Do I look like a resettler?'

'Well, you are looking for housing. I thought...'

'No, I'm a journalist.'

'Ah.'

'What, do I look like a refugee?'

'Hmm. What do refugees look like?'

'Indeed.'

'You go and ask them what they need. We have warm things.'

The village turns out to be located on the edge of Kharkiv, in vacant land alongside the road to the airport, about five hundred metres from the closest permanent housing. The territory, about a quarter of a hectare, is covered with bright metal and plastic modular trailers where nearly four hundred people are living. On the other side of the road, Kharkiv residents have here and there usurped the weed-filled wasteland and created informal vegetable gardens.

'To us, this is a palace,' Lyudmila says.

No matter what, her vital, life-affirming personality makes itself felt.

The twenty-nine-year-old is the mother of three children. The middle one, Maksim, has Down's syndrome. Wherever his mother goes, wherever she stops or sits, the five-year-old boy is right there, hugging her leg.

At home in Antratsyt they lived in a two-storey apartment building that looked like a barracks. Half the apartments were empty even before the war. There was a wooden outhouse and no running water; they carried buckets of water from a well to the second floor. They heated the place with coal: Antratsyt is named after anthracite, a type of coal. They extracted the coal. But it wasn't clean. In order to heat the apartment during the cold season, Lyudmila had to collect four buckets of raw coal by hand every day.

'But here in Kharkiv there's actually a shower! Not in our building, of course, but in the next one over, and you have to stand in line, but at least there is one!'

Lyudmila displays her current palace. While most people's living arrangements in this modular village are based on the dormitory/communal apartment principle – a long hallway with doors onto numerous small rooms – Lyudmila, her husband and their children share two whole, semi-separate rooms. This is because of their disabled child, whose occasional fits make it hard for other children to be in the same space as him.

Lyudmila is sitting on a chair while Maksim hugs her leg. He whimpers occasionally and she strokes his head. Fluorescent lamps, white walls, iron cots and metal lockers, like in a school or gym. And emptiness. They don't have anything to fill even their small space. After all, they left in mid-January in a Gazelle minivan with just a few bags. To buy the tickets, they sold their mobile phones and household appliances cheaply. They drove through Russia, because Ukraine at that time was closed off by checkpoints all along the demarcation line that divided the fighters.

'I thought I'd go crazy. The checkpoints were closed and we couldn't get a pass, you have to be in Ukraine to get a pass. We drove for days. With a disabled child. The driver would stop when necessary. A good man. But it was a van full of people like us. No one wants to be a burden.'

The route Lyudmila and her family took bypassed checkpoints: from Antratsyt into Russia, through Kamensk-Shakhtinsky, Voronezh and Belgorod – and back into Ukraine, to Kharkiv.

'When I finally saw the Ukrainian flag on the border, I nearly cried. We'd made it.'

ARTEM CHAPEYE

This wasn't her first attempt to leave. As soon as 'it all began' (resettlers often talk about the war evasively, in euphemisms, non-judgementally), Lyudmila travelled to Kharkiv without the children, but at the time she wasn't able to find housing. She got registered – and then the MChS (State Service for Emergency Situations) summoned her by phone to the opening of the modular village.

When 'all of this began', Lyudmila initially supported the 'militiamen', as did most of her neighbours. Everyone was watching Russian television, which depicted the change of power in Kyiv after the Euromaidan protests as the coming of a fascist junta. At the time, Right Sector, a group numbering a few hundred people, was mentioned on Russian channels at least as often as United Russia, Russia's ruling party. (Later, in May 2014, only 0.7 per cent voted for Right Sector's leader, who had been heavily promoted by the media in the Ukrainian presidential elections. This was less than a third of the number of votes won by the not-very public businessman with the typically Jewish name Rabinovich, giving rise to sneers at Russian propaganda about 'fascism in Ukraine'. However, the conflict immediately heated up and there were deaths on both sides, so there were real reasons for hostility.)

'Then Cossacks started coming to Antratsyt, and it all began…,' Lyudmila relates.

If, in May 2014, her child's illness was all that stopped her from voting in the home-grown 'referendum' for the autonomy of the 'LNR', which she perceived as a defence against 'fascism', after the arrival of the Cossack organisations, she quickly changed her mind.

'Half our building is pro-Ukraine now, but we only talk about it among ourselves in a whisper. They'd turn us in.'

Lyudmila's family decided to leave not because of the war as such, for Antratsyt itself was fairly calm, but because of the looting, the protection rackets, the way neighbours were 'squeezed' out of their apartments and cars, the constant internal squabbles among the Cossacks and the general poverty.

'Life became intolerable.'

Lyudmila's first husband, the father of her two older children, left her five years ago, right after the birth of the son with Down's syndrome. When she fled, her former husband 'belonged to the LNR militia'.

Back home in Antratsyt, her second husband, Evgeny, who Lyudmila came to the transit village with, had worked in one of the unsanctioned mines, where miners worked off the books and no one guaranteed workers' safety.

The whole time I was in their trailer, Evgeny lay there, turned to the wall, and said nothing. Lyudmila said he was sick. Much later, she said that Evgeny had been depressed for the first few months after the move, because they had no money and he couldn't find work.

'At the hypermarket nearby, there's a notice: "security guards needed". He went and they immediately looked at his passport to see what kind of residence permit he had. "Fine, we'll call you back." A day later they called back. "You don't suit us." And unofficially, "The owner said not to take resettlers. He says they're unreliable, that they'll quit in a month and go back to where they came from."'

Here's Svetlana, one of those who's been lucky when it comes to work. She got a job here as a cleaning woman right away. Her salary is 1,700 hryvnias – the equivalent of sixty euros.

29

ARTEM CHAPEYE

Svetlana has been in Kharkiv since late 2014, so she was one of the first in the transit village. And then she got a job.

When I came the first time and was talking to the administration, Svetlana was actually cleaning. A few times she asked me timidly to move. She'd been ordered to make everything spick and span because they were expecting a visit to the village from the deputy mayor of Kharkiv. Even without tidying up for the special occasion, the village was cleaner than lots of private apartments.

Svetlana suits her name: she's *svetlaya*, 'bright'. She's thirty-four years old. A calm, sweet-looking blonde with grey eyes. She smiles when she talks to me. Even though her town has just been bombed.

She's a single mother. She came from Vuhlehirsk with her daughter, who is seven, and her mother, who has suffered a few strokes. At home, Svetlana worked as a pastry chef. She'd been saving money her whole life for an apartment, and finally bought one a few years before the war.

'In the autumn, the fighting seemed to have ended. Vuhlehirsk was apparently still in Ukraine. I bought a garage cheaply from a neighbour woman. Not that I have a car. But I look ahead.' She smiles at herself. 'If I'd only known. Better to have the money.'

As soon as it became clear, in late 2014, that the DNR and LNR were going to advance on Debaltseve after all, a strategic point under government control not far from Vuhlehirsk, Svetlana gathered up her belongings.

'My daughter's teacher said, "Nothing's going to happen here. Who needs our Vuhlehirsk?" I told her, "Someone does,"' Svetlana says, a defensive, ironic smile on her face.

Svetlana, her daughter and her mother got out on one of

the last trains for Kharkiv. A couple of days later, travel was halted, and soon after that the fighting began, with Vuhlehirsk suffering more than Debaltseve itself.

She watched what was happening to her town on the news.

'Once, I found a video on YouTube. In the dead of winter, two homeless *bomzhiks* are leaving Vuhlehirsk' – Svetlana uses the colloquial word for homeless people, but in an affectionate form. 'They're walking and pulling something on a handcart. A reporter comes up to them to get them to say something. I look, and it's my nephew and … well, another relative!'

As it turned out later, the children had hidden from the shooting in a cellar overnight. A car had been paid to take them to Ukrainian territory in the morning. But they were so frightened they couldn't sleep until the shooting stopped. It was nearly dawn when they fell asleep – and they overslept. The driver drove up to the building and honked, but they didn't hear and didn't come out. The car drove off. In the afternoon, they gathered up what they could on a cart and set out on foot for Yenakiieve, deep in the DNR, just to get away from the front line.

'And I thought they were some kind of *bomzhiks*. Their faces were dirty from the cellar.' Svetlana smiles.

She talks for a long time, calmly, in detail, and with a steady half-smile. When she arrived in Kharkiv, Svetlana was assigned a good-hearted woman in the social protection office, who on her own initiative brought beds into one of the communal spaces designated for housing. Until recently, Svetlana's family had lived in one of the rooms there, among the offices, the state employees and visitors, before they moved here. Now they have one room for the three of them in a dormitory.

'My daughter still doesn't understand that we have nowhere to go back to,' Svetlana says. 'She's constantly saying, "Now,

when we go back … Let's go mushroom picking again, okay?"
She remembers her toys…'

Svetlana is silent, then says, 'It was such a quiet town.
I adored it.'

To her own surprise she starts sobbing, covers her face
with her hands, and for a long time can't stop. She takes deep,
ragged breaths to calm herself down, tries to speak – and starts
sobbing again.

Looking back, I often think that Svetlana's lament was the main
reason I left journalism more than a year ago. Next to you
someone is convulsed in sobs, and you're sitting there frozen
and don't know what to do or what even can be done. If I were
a woman, I could at least hug her. As it is, you sit there perfectly
still, very tall, feeling like you're trying to swallow a stone, and
all you can do is murmur something like, 'Come, come now…'

I stopped writing with a vague feeling of guilt because
Svetlana, Lyudmila and the other resettlers I knew couldn't
run away from their life and I could. It was too hard. I've been
interrogated and beaten, and I've come under fire from Grad
multiple rocket launchers, but constantly encountering sorrow
turned out to be harder.

A fifty-year-old violinist from Luhansk stands in line for humanitarian aid and tells a psychologist in a choking voice that
taking is a lot harder than giving. A sixty-year-old woman tells
the story of how she fled a town under government control
and now has no right to assistance, even though an army
unit is posted near her building and she's afraid of return
fire from insurgents. In a whisper, as if it were a secret, she
says, 'It doesn't matter whose shells you die from – it's equally

frightening.' A pensioner standing in line for her ration in Kramatorsk, which has only just been fired upon by insurgents, weeps quietly because at that very moment the Ukrainian army is firing on her home town of Horlivka. Naturally, the Ukrainian authorities constantly deny firing on residential blocks. But the insurgents are shooting at army positions that are using the civilian population as shields, so the army fires back at the insurgents. A very old grandmother from Lutuhyne, who is weaving camouflage nets for the army in a dark hallway, wipes her eyes with the back of her hand and says, 'Maidan carved up families. I haven't had anything to do with my sister for six months.' A resettler from Donetsk, a large grown man, looks up at the ceiling to keep the tears from falling when he says he's stopped speaking to his own parents.

Even the volunteers helping the internal refugees, despite their active compassion, often display an emotional detachment. They try to bureaucratise assistance.

Marina Alferova, director of Station Kharkiv in Izium, says, 'We have a psychologist for the resettlers, and now she herself needs a psychologist. The majority of our volunteers are resettlers themselves, and I'm constantly telling them, "Give out what you're supposed to on the list, but you don't need to ask questions or get close to them or pity them. That would be too much to bear."'

Alferova shows me a photo of a five-year-old girl who was recently brought out from the firing. It's hard to look into the child's eyes even in the photograph.

But of course it's impossible to run away from all of this. Knowing so many resettlers, you're constantly seeing new ones around you. They're everywhere. You call a taxi and the car has Donetsk plates. Driving a taxi is one of the few jobs you can get, no matter what your background is, and providing you still have a vehicle. At the second-hand shop you hear a woman on her mobile phone, digging through the old clothing, discussing registration and attempts to get her child into day care. At a children's dance, two respectable-looking parents talk about the situation in Donetsk, naming specific streets and neighbourhoods. A journalist colleague, it turns out, underwent torture in Luhansk on suspicion of spying. My wife sends used clothing by the bagful to a woman resettler in Cherkasy Oblast, who makes a living there by reselling old things. One of our closest friends, the writer Vladimir Rafeyenko, from Donetsk, has even become a resettler.

At the same time, you periodically see discrimination and negative attitudes shown towards internal refugees. Or I may just be overly sensitive. Certainly not everyone is biased against the resettlers. But I imagine even the resettlers can't fail to notice episodes such as the following:

In Ivano-Frankivsk Oblast, most of the media rebroadcasts supposed 'news' about 'goons with chains' from Donbass allegedly being thrown out of a hotel for being rude to their hosts, but when I go to report on it, the story turns out to be pure folklore.

A teenager from Kharkiv who is couch-surfing at our house tells us about the uptick in bicycle thefts, and even though there's no proof of it, he's sure the resettlers are to blame.

In our neighbourhood, car batteries are constantly being stolen. When I become a victim, my neighbour tries to convince me that of course the resettlers are to blame, these former professional miners have retrained as professional thieves.

Except that the refugees have been here for years, and the situation has only deteriorated in the last few months. The police officers I call link this to the recent 'Savchenko law', under which tens of thousands of people incarcerated before the war were released from prison simultaneously.

Most often you hear that the resettlers 'have only themselves to blame' for what has happened to them, that they brought Grads down on their own heads. Yes, it's because of the resettlers that Russia is supplying weapons to insurgents, including the fairly powerful weapon that did for Malaysian Airlines flight MH17. Yes, the residents of Donbass 'conjured up Putin themselves', a resettler named Rafeyenko says sarcastically.

What can I say? Some citizens envy the internal refugees. In a country where, according to UN data, a third of people live below the poverty line, the resettlers get as much as 400 hryvnias (approximately thirteen euros) a month from the state.

Transit villages like the one in Kharkiv have also popped up in Zaporizhia and Dnipro. An article recently appeared in the Ukrainian media about one of these villages, depicting its inhabitants as lumpen elements living at other people's expense and the village itself as a 'ghetto'. A place where a problem had settled. A 'problem', not people.

While I was preparing my report, one of the (remote) administrative organisers of the modular village in Kharkiv told me, 'I'm sharing my opinions with you not as a representative of the organisation, but as the way I see it. And the way it is' – he felt it necessary to add. 'Some of the people there work, but very few. Most just sit around and wait for assistance, believing they're entitled to it. They have no plans to integrate themselves anywhere.' He then used the same epithet as the journalists in that article: 'The fact is, it's a ghetto.'

.   .   .

The village on the edge of Kharkiv is now wholly the financial responsibility of the local authorities. Outwardly, only minor changes have occurred over the last year and a half: a blue mesh fence around the perimeter and a new playground. It still says that this is a 'transit' village intended for the 'temporary' placement of internally displaced people.

But most of the faces are familiar to me. These are the same people I saw a year and a half ago. There's a short line outside one of the barracks, exclusively women.

'Good Samaritans from Kharkiv are giving out food baskets,' Lyudmila explains.

She and her family are still here. Her disabled son, Maksim, who has now reached school age, has been assigned to a special institution where he'll go to school with children who have similar problems. Her husband, Evgeny, eventually did find a job. He stopped going to the hypermarket where they wouldn't hire him, even though they always had signs up about openings. Instead, he worked for the municipal security service and then found a job as a security guard at another shopping centre nearby: 3,500 hryvnias a month (approximately 120 euros), and shifts every third day.

'My husband likes it. Between shifts he finds odd jobs. And they've just raised his pay a fair bit.' Lyudmila immediately moves on to the main subject now worrying everyone. 'I used to pay 600 hryvnias, but now it's 1,800.'

The municipal authorities have told the resettlers that the increase in fees is due to the rise in prices for utilities, although they get more for these services in the living spaces here than they do from people in private apartments. What the resettlers are paying now is starting to look like rent. The amounts are still less than they would be for renting even a one-room apartment in Kharkiv, which is why people stay. But many people in the village, though not all, expect further price increases, and they have good reason to suspect this. According to unofficial reports, the town hall is of the opinion that the people in the transit village should be evicted somehow.

'Some people envy us,' Lyudmila says. 'I understand. There are a lot of poor people in Kharkiv. Right now everyone's utilities have gone up. I understand that perfectly. But envy us? When I hear that, I say, "At least you're living at home."'

Lyudmila now pays an additional amount for two 'extra' places in her trailer. If she didn't do that, they'd put another family in with them. Resettlers are talking about the coming 'densification'.

'Can you imagine? Living with strangers, especially with my Maksim? As it is, you hear every cough through the wall. Everyone's been getting on everyone else's nerves for a long time. It's understandable. There are all kinds of people here and they don't always get along easily.'

Lyudmila's family has no plans to go back to Antratsyt.

'My husband went back to collect our things. Naturally he lay down on our bed to rest. He said it was quiet. He couldn't hear anyone through the wall. And those are our home walls, after all. But go back? Where? First of all, I don't recognise that government. There is a country called Ukraine. And there's Russia. But there is no Novorossiya. And second of all, I think you've heard about the way they've started going after the resettlers. You've heard, right? If they come to check up on me and I'm not here, they'll cut off all my payments. I could understand if it were only the "resettler payments". That would be fair. But they're cutting off everything – people's old-age and disability pensions. They would cut off the care assistance for my disabled child. If only there were a court that would recognise that this is unconstitutional. ... We're Ukrainian citizens, after all.'

Lyudmila says she's planning to rent separate housing in Kharkiv. But not right now. Once spring comes. It's terrible to move anywhere with children in winter.

Svetlana from Vuhlehirsk is still living here after a year and a half.

'You probably remember, I was working as a cleaner? But a little while ago I lost my job. After they raised our pay.'

Her pay (1,700 hryvnias, raised to 2,000 in the last few months) barely covered the new housing cost in the village (1,400 hryvnias). Svetlana is afraid of densification too, so she's paying conscientiously. She's looking for a better-paid job now.

'I'm a cook by training. I've worked as a seamstress. I'm not worried. I'll find a job.' She smiles.

The problem isn't a job as such, it's the schedule. Her daughter has to be picked up from school at two in the afternoon. And her old mother can barely walk and needs care.

Svetlana's mother recently had to go to hospital because of complications after her latest stroke and rheumatism of the joints. When the doctor in charge found out the woman was a resettler, he refused to admit her to hospital. Medicine in Ukraine is free in theory, but in practice patients have to buy all their own medicines and syringes.

'The doctor thought that if mama was a resettler, she wouldn't be able to pay.'

But her mother threatened him with the telephone number she had written down of a Kharkiv city official, and the doctor relented. He would admit her if the family paid for all her medicines in advance. Svetlana names a figure equal to three months' wages. When I ask how they were able to pay so much at once, she smiles.

'We agreed to buy the medicines gradually, as and when they're needed. We're stringing them along.'

Svetlana's daughter is already in third grade. She talks about their home in Vuhlehirsk less often. She walks in, sits close to her mother and listens to the conversation.

'Are the Samaritans already distributing things?' Svetlana asks her daughter.

'Not yet. They said they'd start soon,' her daughter says impatiently.

Her light brown hair is braided. Freckles on her nose, like her mother. Light eyes, like her mother. The child watches the adults closely, listening to their conversation.

'Okay, go and stand in line.' Svetlana sends her off.

When her daughter leaves, reluctantly, Svetlana says, 'I went home. We have a five-storey building there, brick. The fifth and fourth storeys have come down. My apartment is on the second floor, and it survived; the windows have been smashed, that's all. But the stairs in the entry are warped and walking on them is dangerous. After the shooting, the plumbing broke and everything was flooded. The parquet swelled up and there are damp spots on the walls. My brother stayed on, you see. I took him there and showed him the apartment. He said it wasn't worth repairing.'

'Your brother's building wasn't bombed?'

'It was.' That half-smile of Svetlana's now wanders across her face. 'But not too badly. And he has a private sector residence. He's adding to it little by little.'

'You didn't think to move in with him?'

'He has three kids.' She grins. 'How can we dump ourselves on him?'

Despite the higher costs in the transit village, Svetlana can't bring herself even to look for other housing.

'You never know who you're going to end up with. We don't have any savings. What if the landlord asked us to leave in a month? Where would we go then?'

DREAMS DEFERRED

LIVING IN LIMBO IN DADAAB, THE
WORLD'S LARGEST REFUGEE CAMP

ABDI LATIF DAHIR

The journalist ABDI LATIF DAHIR was born in Kenya but grew up in the Somali capital, Mogadishu. Abdi studied at the United States International University – Africa in Nairobi and earned his master's degree from Columbia University. Abdi works as a reporter with *Quartz*, a digitally native news outlet that is a guide to the new global economy.

I T was a cool morning in Dadaab, the world's largest refugee camp. Amphile Kassim sat cross-legged on a thin mattress at his home, pondering the past as he stroked his red-hennaed goatee. Amphile, popularly known as Anfi, spoke about the day when, as a ten-year-old, he first became a refugee. Anfi, an ethnic Somali, and his family fled clashes in their home town in the Bale zone of what is now the Oromia region of Ethiopia. It was 1974 and Anfi, alongside his parents and siblings, sought asylum in neighbouring Somalia. After the central government in that country was toppled in 1991, he and his family left again, this time for Kenya, where they were granted asylum and settled in the Dadaab refugee camp.

For more than two and a half decades, the Dadaab refugee camp has marked the beginning and the end of Anfi's story: a dusty outpost in north-eastern Kenya that welcomed its first inhabitants when Somalia's government dissolved and a congeries of factions wrought havoc across the country. Since then, Dadaab has grown to become the world's largest refugee complex, at one point hosting over 600,000 people displaced from more than a dozen countries. The refugees are dispersed across five camps located in just under a twenty-mile stretch. Ethnic Somalis like Anfi make up 95 per cent of those refugees, with the latest numbers from the UNHCR showing over 260,000 Somalis call the place home.

The sun was starting to crack through the mud and stick house that has been Anfi's home for years, turning the shades of morning into day. Anfi had an imperturbable tranquillity about him. His demeanour was like an unrung bell; one could never be sure of what he would say next, or which event from the past he would recall. When his family set off for Somalia from Ethiopia that fateful morning, he reflected, 'I never thought I would be a refugee for this long.' Officially, he is now a fifty-two-year-old man who has spent the last four decades of his life as a refugee – running, relocating and waiting. Through it all, he said, he'd relinquished all hope of ever going back home. He repeatedly stated that he had pledged his allegiance to the UNHCR, which oversees the camp, as 'my government', its white-and-blue logo as 'my flag', and the refugee camps as 'my only country'.

But if Anfi was clear-eyed about the past, he definitely wasn't about the future. After more than two decades of effusive warmth towards refugees, a cold front was enveloping Dadaab. In November 2013, the Kenyan government signed, together with the Somali government and the UN Refugee Agency, a tripartite agreement to repatriate Somali refugees in Kenya on a voluntary basis. The impetus behind the agreement was the build-up of a series of events from 2008 to 2011, when renewed conflict and severe drought led tens of thousands of Somalis to cross the border and seek relief in Dadaab. The 2011 drought was especially catastrophic, leading to the death of almost five per cent of the entire Somali population and warranting more than a billion dollars in aid efforts.

At the height of relief efforts in October 2011, two staff members working for the humanitarian agency Médecins Sans Frontières were kidnapped from Dadaab. A few days later, Kenya's army invaded Somalia in order to mount an attack against Al-Shabaab, the Somali terrorist group that reportedly carried out the abduction. Over the next few years,

Al-Shabaab responded with deadly force, carrying out attacks across Kenya that targeted churches, bus stations and nightclubs. In September 2013, the group carried out a deadly attack, killing sixty-seven people at the upmarket Westgate Mall in Nairobi. Immediately afterwards, officials in the Kenyan government called for the closure of Dadaab, labelling it a breeding ground and 'nursery for terrorists'.

This was followed by the launch of Operation Usalama Watch (Peace Watch) in April 2014, which led to the rounding up of almost four thousand people of Somali descent, mostly refugees, residing in urban areas. The operation, aimed at flushing out illegal immigrants and Al-Shabaab sympathisers, was mostly carried out in Somali-populated neighbourhoods in the capital, Nairobi. Those apprehended were held in detention centres that were labelled as 'concentration camps', in conditions described as reminiscent of British gulag camps in Kenya in the 1950s, when the colonial government detained, tortured and abused Kenyans agitating for independence. Dozens of Somali refugees were deported back to Somalia after being summarily held and without appearing in a court of law, according to Human Rights Watch.

Eight months later, on 8 December 2014, the UNHCR started the pilot phase of the project aimed at repatriating Somali refugees in Kenya. The agency called the process 'a significant step to address the needs for lasting solutions to one of the world's most protracted refugee situations'. Ten days later, a fist fight broke out on the floor of Kenya's parliament – broadcast nationally – as legislators passed a controversial and wide-ranging security law. Several provisions in the law were aimed at capping the total number of refugees living in the country to 150,000 – there were 600,000 at the time – and limiting the movement of refugees to designated camps. Human rights groups cast this as a cautionary tale that implied that the refugees could be forcibly returned, thus contravening national, continental and international laws pertaining to the protection of refugees. While High Court judges later declared the previous conditions unconstitutional, they nonetheless upheld parts of the law that placed restrictions on the movement of refugees within Kenya.

This was further compounded by an attack at the Garissa University College in north-eastern Kenya on 2 April 2015. Al-Shabaab militants killed 148 people, most of them students, in a deadly dawn raid that occurred just seventy miles from the Dadaab refugee camp. After this episode, Kenya's deputy president William Ruto called for the camp to be closed within three months and for all refugees to be relocated. 'The way America changed after 9/11 is the way Kenya will change after Garissa,' Ruto announced in a statement.

After the Garissa University attack, said Anfi, the events of the last few years fused to create a tale of hardship in Dadaab: rising insecurity, lack of proper sanitation, outbreaks of disease and police harassment, combined with a sense of foreboding about what the repatriation process would mean for his family's future. As these events unfolded, humanitarian agencies, including the World Food Programme, announced they were reducing food and aid rations due to dwindling funds. For decades, humanitarian agencies and foreign donor governments had sponsored operations in Dadaab with little or no burden falling upon the Kenyan government. The government's encampment policy, however, had left the refugees with few, if any, options to decrease their dependency on aid and create sustainable livelihoods.

'We feel like we are in a warehouse,' he said. 'There's no movement. We are just seated in one place. It's like a prison.'

Now Anfi and hundreds of thousands of refugees like him are worried about what the place they have called home for decades will become in the next few years. In early May 2016, the Kenyan government disbanded the Department of Refugee Affairs (DRA), the government agency that registered and managed refugees, paving the way for the closure of the Dadaab camp. It was a crossroads moment and Anfi worried about his wife, whom he married before moving to Kenya, and their children. His frustrations almost weaved into a conspiracy: he alleged that authorities overseeing the camp were working against the refugees, deliberately cutting back basic services to pressure them to leave.

'Where do I go back to?' Anfi said, throwing his long arms and scrawny fingers up in the air. 'I have nothing to go back to.'

To get to Dadaab, one had to get clearance from the DRA, the now-disbanded government agency that once oversaw the registration of all refugees and asylum seekers in Kenya. The DRA's office was located in the quiet Nairobi suburb of Lavington, at a house called the Castle, whose architecture is reminiscent of a colonial fort. It has large imposing windows, expansive rooms, and an eerie, quiet feel. When I visited in December 2015, I couldn't help but notice the discrepancy between the building's grandiose façade and the people it was meant to serve. There were calendars with kitsch graphic designs hanging on the walls, displaying the agency's motto: Refugees are people.

After I received my clearance form, I rode on an early-morning bus from Nairobi heading to Garissa town. Garissa

47

is the administrative centre that oversees the six constituencies that make up Garissa county; Dadaab is one of them. The bus, which was speeding, was decorated with religious paraphernalia and stock photos that declared 'There's no God but Allah' and had phrases celebrating Islamic holidays. After six hours of driving through central Kenya's green and misty highlands, we crossed over to the barren land and hot climate of Garissa. Located just 220 miles from Nairobi, Garissa is a booming, congested township that Interpol once deemed the safest town in East and Central Africa. I slept in Garissa for the night, before proceeding the next morning to Dadaab.

The Google Maps app will inform you that the distance between Garissa and Dadaab can be covered in an hour and twenty-five minutes by car. Instead, it is a three-and-a-half-hour drive through monotonous terrain, strewn with acacia and shrubs and with no landmarks. The only measure of familiarity on these deserted roads is the hearty exchange of greetings between drivers who stop their cars to say hello, or who drive fast past each other while honking. The scenes whizzing by are of unnerving banality, full of sleepy hamlets where mothers holding their naked children peer at passing cars from under the shade of trees. Young girls, standing nearby, rush towards buses and commercial trucks, hoping they will stop for passengers to buy camel and goat milk packaged in used plastic bottles.

Before completing the trip to Dadaab, my driver, my fixer and I stopped in the small village of Hagar Buul. We were seated inside a shed, where a solar-powered television was on. Four men were chewing khat, a mildly stimulating plant. They were drinking tea and watching Fox News's Sean Hannity talking about Bernie Sanders, the Democratic presidential candidate. The men had chapped lips and dusty legs, and each one had a dagger and a walking stick placed not far from him. 'This old man should win,' one of the men said, referring to Sanders. He had a bulge in his cheek from stuffing the khat in his mouth. 'No, no,' a man sitting to his right, clearly not feeling the Bern, said. 'The lady should win. She deserves it.' They got into a kerfuffle about leadership, women and American democracy, and soon enough, the Sanders supporter who held the remote control started flipping channels. He finally settled on the Russia Today channel, which was advertising a documentary about members of Kenya's Maasai community visiting Russia, titled *Maasai: From Sand to Snow*. Shortly afterwards, we left the men to their khat. We drove speeding through the difficult terrain and emerged from winding, labyrinthine and sandy lanes to reach Dadaab town at around six o'clock in the evening.

Dadaab is a refugee complex divided into five camps. There's Hagadera, Dagahley and Ifo, which hosted the first wave of refugees who arrived in 1991. Then there are the more recent Ifo 2 and Kambios camps, constructed for new arrivals in July and September 2011 respectively. Each of the camps is divided into sections that are named in alphabetical order. Each section is divided into blocks, and each block has its own community leaders, a playground, health clinics, mosques and a tap stand for collecting water. Some houses are built with corrugated iron and sticks and others with stones, but they almost all feature a tarp. There are bustling markets, especially those in the Hagadera and Dagahley camps, which sell cheap utensils, textiles and toys. There are pharmacies, banks, restaurants, money transfer agencies, technology shops and meat-selling vendors pitched right next to barber shops and salons. Over the years, Dadaab has developed into a town, a remote outpost with a geographical outline that looks like a lazy, slouching L-shape when viewed on a map.

Across the camps, billboards describe methods to prevent the spread of cholera, HIV and a slew of other diseases. NGOs advertise their work on metallic boards with verbs as predicates describing their activities: supplementing, rehabilitating, implementing and supporting projects in Dadaab. An endless list of NGOs dots the Dadaab landscape: the International Rescue Committee, Norwegian Refugee Council, World Food Programme, Lutheran World Federation, International Organization for Migration, African Development Solutions, and many more. The organisations' combined efforts have made Dadaab a federal city that offers its stateless residents the perks of education, health and water, as well as economic opportunities. Twenty-five years since it was first established, Dadaab has morphed into a permanent home for many – a self-styled refugee republic for people locked in a cycle of waiting and waiting.

Between December 2014 and October 2016, a total of 33,000 Somalis were repatriated from Kenya to more than thirty-one locations across Somalia. For the Somali refugees, the repatriation wasn't a popular idea: a joint UNHCR–IOM survey carried out in 2014 concluded that only 2.6 per cent of the refugees living in Dadaab wanted to return. The response was positive among the refugees who arrived in Kenya after the start of this millennium, who were more confident of returning to their properties or had access to relatives or friends who would assist them with rent or accommodation. Those like Anfi, who arrived in the early 1990s, said they didn't want to go back because they didn't feel they would have access to viable economic opportunities.

Kenya's threat to close the camp was in total variance with the voluntary nature of the tripartite agreement entered into by Kenya, Somalia and the UNHCR. The fifteen-page document notes that no matter what, Kenya will continue to provide protection and assistance to all refugees until a long-lasting resolution is attained – that is, until peace is achieved in Somalia. Looked at from that angle, the tripartite agreement seems a weak pact. It is based on assumptions – security in Somalia is improving; Kenya has suffered a heavy economic and security burden in hosting the refugees – rather than focusing on the volatile and unpredictable circumstances that would face returnees on the ground. For the refugees, deciding to go back to Somalia is like striking a Faustian bargain, but without getting anything at their end. Somalia, for one, faces more critical and complex problems than it faced a decade or two ago. Food insecurity threatens millions due to a prolonged lack of rainfall linked to climate change. Terrorist attacks carried out by Al-Shabaab have become a mainstay across cities and towns in Somalia. Corruption and poor management of public finances have also bedevilled Somalia's internationally-backed central government. This is not to mention the real-life, game of thrones politics playing out across the country's federal states.

However, according to legal analysts, for all its weak provisions, the tripartite agreement is a progressive document that, on paper, takes into account the needs of refugees who are willing to go back. It prevents involuntary separation of family members; makes sure that refugees have the proper education, birth, marriage and divorce papers; ensures that children, women and the elderly receive adequate support during reintegration; exempts tax from personal and communal wealth accumulated over the years; and mandates the Somali government to expedite residency status for any non-Somali members of a family.

The agreement 'contributes to some sort of progression', says Andrew Maina, who works as a programme officer with the Refugee Consortium of Kenya, an NGO that works to protect refugees and stateless people in Kenya. 'It is not [just] basically going home that is the agenda; it is going home in safety and dignity.'

The process of repatriation starts when a refugee household arrives at one of several designated return helpdesks across the five camps. These desks are arranged in a three-tier way: the UNHCR acts as the lead agency that facilitates the return, seconded by the Norwegian Refugee Council, which provides information on areas of return, and ending with Kenya's DRA desk, which authorises travel documentation for the refugees. The entire process takes up to a week. This, UN officials say, is enough time for returnees to discuss with friends and notify family members of their decision to go back.

But for some refugees who have been in Dadaab refugee camp for a long time, the swiftness with which the process is carried out is a major downside. One afternoon, while paying my lunch bill at Midnimo Restaurant in the Hagadera camp, I asked the cashier about his take on the repatriation plan. He told me he had six children; the eldest was thirteen years old. He said he wasn't planning to go back, but even if he decided to go, the adjustment would be too problematic for his family. 'My kids don't know Somalia,' he said. 'I can't start this conversation with them now.'

When I countered that it was tough to be in a refugee camp for more than two and a half decades, and perhaps it would prove better to go back to Somalia, he started shaking his head. 'In Kenya we are refugees. If you go [back to Somalia], you become a refugee in your own country,' he said. His plan wasn't to look back, but instead to go forward. 'I have hope that I will be resettled. I want to go to America,' he said.

To help the residents of Dadaab get used to the idea of going back to Somalia, the UNHCR organised 'go and see' and 'come and tell' visits for a group of selected refugees. The teams, comprising twenty or thirty people, visited cities like Mogadishu and Kismayo, and came back to the camp to share their findings with fellow refugees. Somali government officials received them in Somalia and helped them visit schools, hospitals and government departments, besides organising meetings with businessmen, youth and women's groups.

Aden Rashid, a repatriation officer with the UNHCR, said this was all part of an effort to provide information to the Somali refugees, not to actively promote returns to Somalia. The UN, he said, was aware of the fragility of the situation in the country and would not actively encourage refugees to go back. The visit, he said, was part of their strategy to let the refugees tell their own story and share their experience of visiting Somalia after such a long time.

Hawa Abdi Mohamed, a community leader who lives in Dagahley, was part of a group that visited Kismayo in November 2015. Hawa herself fled the city and came to Kenya as a refugee in 1992. She has given birth to thirteen children – three of whom died – while living in the camp. Riding in a government convoy, the group visited the Kismayo port, once a profitable commercial hub for Al-Shabaab. They toured the city's international airport, visited health and educational institutions, and assessed the possibility of returning to Kismayo. But Hawa couldn't recognise the city she knew as a young woman and recoiled at the thought of the level of destruction in it. The semblance of stability there, she said, was confined to the borders of Kismayo town, with anything beyond it dangerous and inaccessible.

One afternoon, during the group's stay in Kismayo, a succession of gunshots rang out in the air from close by. A lady in Mohamed's group started running around in fear, until someone yelled at her to duck for cover. Thinking about it now, Hawa giggled at the memory and exclaimed in dismay how she had forgotten the sound of war and got used to relative peace in Dadaab.

During the Kismayo visit, she also thought of her own children's safety, specifically that of her eldest daughter, who has four children of her own and is pregnant with a fifth. 'I couldn't recognise Kismayo. So what about my daughter?' she wondered. Her children love Kenya, the country where they grew up, and the dilemma was that they didn't know anything about Somalia.

It wasn't lost on Hawa that her children and grandchildren were first and foremost refugees: Somalis living in a country whose collective disposition of late was not receptive and accommodative to people like them. Within Kenyan society, public opinion has experienced the polarisation of being either humanitarian and welcoming towards the refugees, or vehemently calling for them to be expelled. Influential columnists have called Dadaab 'a dangerous staging post' and called for the 'aliens idling' in Dadaab to be expelled and the camp promptly closed. Al-Shabaab's repeated targeting of Christians in Kenya has also tugged at the heart of a predominantly Christian nation hosting predominantly Muslim refugees. This has inadvertently given the refugee issue a religious dimension and underpins the debate on how religious harmony can be sustained.

'We think of this repatriation day and night,' Mohamed said, staring at the sandy ground. She wiped sweat from her face with the ends of her long, pink jilbab. She said that what she'd seen in Kismayo made her strongly believe in her earlier conviction: that the timing of the repatriation process would not be propitious. 'It's like choosing the lesser of two evils.'

Young or old, man or woman, people's stories in Dadaab are told in fragments, narrated in the form of a patchwork of memories about a brutal war, a lost relative, a ruined home and a hankering for a country mired in conflict. A chorus of fatalism is almost always present in the threads of these stories. Accounts are familiar on the whole, yet dissimilar in their specifics. The refugees put on a mask of stoicism and sturdiness even though they admit to their own vulnerabilities. Some, like Anfi and Hawa, are old enough to remember what they lost. Others, born and bred in Dadaab, are young enough to know only the trap that has caught them and the precariousness with which they are building their future.

During my visit, radio stations played and replayed sponsored public service announcements extolling the benefits of going back to Somalia. Walking through Dadaab, you notice empty courtyards, proof that neighbours have decided to leave. Conversation in mosques was about how an aunt, a friend or a brother was vacillating between going and staying.

Somali refugees I spoke to were incredulous about rumours regarding repatriation, about any information coming from Somalia. They worried about the economic and social bonds they had established over decades, and whether they were ready to abjure the realm and leave Kenya for good. The repatriation process, many said, was presented to them as a fait accompli, and now they just had to watch and see it unfold.

I asked Anfi if he had thought about leaving the Dadaab refugee camp. He said he had considered going to Borama, a city in the autonomous region of Somaliland in north-western Somalia; he had friends there and would be able to get work.

Would he consider going back to Ethiopia where he was born, I asked.

His answer came out of his mouth like dragon fire: 'No! No! No!' He said that he got goosebumps after I asked him that question, and gave me a serious look. A few minutes later, he was emphatically opposed to leaving the camp at all.

Despite the hard conditions in the camp, Anfi clung to what was great about his life. He thought of his grandchildren, his son who had just finished high school, his daughter who was about to get married. He enjoyed his work as a vaccination nurse, which he had done for decades with different organisations. He got up and brought back certificates of recommendation from Médecins Sans Frontières officials, which described him as an honest, flexible, reliable and hardworking employee, from when he worked at a health post in Dagahley.

'Sometimes, death is better than life,' Anfi concluded. He said he really hoped that his family's resettlement plan to the United States would go through soon.

He looked downcast, and fondly touched the certificates of recommendation. Clouds were gathering in the sky and the blue horizon was turning dishwater grey.

'It's a very, very tough issue,' Anfi said. 'But Allah will open a door for us.'

SOURCES:

www.fews.net; www.aljazeera.com; www.standardmedia.co.ke; www.bbc.co.uk; www.hrw.org; www.unhcr.org; www.nation.co.ke; www.reuters.com; www1.wfp.org; garissa.go.ke; www.the-star.co.ke; www.refworld.org; www.securitycouncilreport.org; www.chathamhouse.org

ANTHROPOPHAGISTS STILL

ANDRÉA DEL FUEGO

Translated from the Portuguese by Jethro Soutar

The Brazilian author ANDREA DEL FUEGO was born in 1975 in São Paulo, where she later studied Philosophy and where she still lives today. As well as a range of children's books, short stories and contributions to different anthologies, she is also the author of the highly successful novel *Os Malaquais* [The Malaquias] (2010), which has been translated into numerous languages and won the José Saramago Prize. Her latest novel is called *As Minaturas* [The Miniatures] (2013).

JETHRO SOUTAR is a translator of Spanish and Portuguese. He has translated novels from Argentina, Brazil and Guinea-Bissau, and *By Night the Mountain Burns* and *The Gurugu Pledge* by Juan Tomás Ávila Laurel from Equatorial Guinea. He is a co-founder of Ragpicker Press and Editor of Dedalus Africa.

S ão Paulo has absorbed more immigrants than any other Brazilian city. Some four-and-a-half million foreigners came to Brazil in the mid-nineteenth century, three million of them arriving via the port of Santos and bound for São Paulo. In 1886, Brazil even formed an association aimed at encouraging families to move to São Paulo. Two years later, the Hospedaria dos Imigrantes (Immigrants' Hostel) opened, and would operate until 1978 as a city-centre establishment providing new arrivals with doctors, meals, lodgings for up to eight days and contact with employers hiring manual labour. What we now traditionally call 'Paulistano' (being of or from the city of São Paulo) really refers to an amalgamation of cultures, with some seventy-plus nationalities currently registered as inhabitants of the city. The Germans were the first immigrants to arrive, in 1827, introducing classical music and, in commercial terms, producing beer and paper. The Italians came next, bringing lyric song and opera, making major contributions to modernism via Victor Brecheret and Alfredo Volpi, and commercially dominating the shoemaking and coppersmith trades. The Japanese arrived in 1908 and built an entire city-centre neighbourhood that retains its own particular identity to this day. Jews brought high-quality fabrics and settled where their customers lived, in neighbourhoods such as Higienópolis, home to the coffee barons. Arabs came with rice, aubergines and oranges, hawking their wares in the city centre (as ever) in an area that is now the most popular commercial district in town, hundreds of buses bringing shoppers from all over Brazil every day. The city's first sports clubs were founded by Arabs: Monte Líbano ('Mount Lebanon') and Esporte Clube Sírio ('Syrian Sports Club').

In 1922, Mario de Andrade published his seminal poetry collection *Hallucinated City* (entitled *Paulicéia Desvairada* in Portuguese). He was one of the intellectual architects of Brazilian Modernism and it was in his house that the 'Anthropophagy Manifesto' was first read in 1928, as penned by the principal cultural polemicist of the era, Oswald de Andrade (no relation to Mario). Naturally the house was in the city centre, a nucleus from which neighbourhoods, suburbs and peripheries would radiate, today home to some twelve million people. The 'Anthropophagy Manifesto' shaped not so much an artistic cause as a city's destiny.

> Only ANTHROPOPHAGY unites us. Socially. Economically. Philosophically. The world's one true law. The hidden expression in every individualism, every collectivism. In every religion. In every peace treaty. Tupi or not tupi, that is the question.
>
> (OSWALD DE ANDRADE, *REVISTA DE ANTROPOFAGIA* [*ANTHROPOPHAGY MAGAZINE*], MAY 1928)

Anthropophagy was here already, of course. Amerigo Vespucci, a Florentine explorer, claimed to have witnessed a cannibalistic ritual in Rio Grande do Norte in 1501, the victim a European man. The ceremony revolved around eating the prisoner's flesh, but only after he'd been admitted into the tribe, a custom the Tupi also kept. Another traveller, Tommaso Garzoni, wrote that the same tribe ate their dead relatives, for a human stomach was thought to be a more dignified resting place than a worm's. In 1555, the first bishop of Brazil was eaten by the Caetés, the bishop having cautioned the Portuguese against acquiring indigenous customs such as smoking, before himself being duly roasted and served. The 'Anthropophagy Manifesto' claimed that Brazilian national identity was the result of devouring and digesting indigenous, African and European cultures, and whatever else besides. It argued that the digestive system filters substances deemed beneficial to the organism, ingredients which in this case were cultural, and had the paradoxical effect of producing a cuisine in which all the various human compo-nents are identifiable, the gastronomic smorgasbord that São Paulo is famous for. After a few years of adaptation, immigrants will adjust their clothing, reduce their religious practices and listen to local music, but their cooking will remain unchanged.

São Paulo seems to be the Brazilian city that has best man-aged to culturally digest its different peoples, whether they came on ships in the nineteenth century or were trafficked on buses and planes by 'coyotes' in the twenty-first, as is the case with many Haitians. In a sense, the city's Modern Art Week celebrates the hotchpotch, all the continents thrown into a caul-dron and cooked on a low yet constant heat. The recent intake of refugees – from across Latin America, the Middle East and Africa – provides but the latest layer in the city's cultural fabric, previous layers having long become sediment, a phenomenon that is unprecedented only to untrained eyes. Keen to explore this latest layer, I begin my search in my own neighbourhood.

There's a record shop on my block that sells craft beer and food barbecued in the backyard. For several months it has promoted a Refugee Supper, whereby Palestinians prepare falafel and *saj*, a bread cooked to order and stuffed with fragrant meat. When I told the shop's owner about the piece I was writing he said

I should come along, but not bring a camera; he tries to protect the refugees from excessive media prying. I arrive early and approach Mohamad, who came to Brazil a year ago, via Syria. Mohamad and his son cook the main meal for the Refugee Supper, in a yard serving as a kitchen, with views to the west of the city where most of São Paulo's artists and intellectuals live. Mohamad has a relaxed face, with the odd missing tooth, but his son, who arrived in Brazil not three weeks ago, is visibly frustrated at not being able to understand what I'm saying. His shoulders slump, so I soften my questions, shape them as comments and not enquiries. Mohamad and his son speak Arabic to one another, but chance a little Portuguese to tell me how long it will be until the falafel is ready: *cinco minuta.* I want to know if he's Muslim, where his wife is, whether his son has a girlfriend, whether he has any grandchildren. What did he leave behind in Palestine? Questions pop into my head, superimposing themselves over news agency footage, the scripted film that is 24-hour CNN. It's still early; they're lighting the coals to cook the meat seasoned with cinnamon, pepper and a secret ingredient, and have yet to heat the oil for the meatballs. Mohamad's son could be any Brazilian kid travelling home on the metro, just as he could be a face on CNN, some lad carrying a wounded body. Aiman arrives a little later, a Palestinian who speaks fluent Portuguese, to install a cash register in this makeshift restaurant by draping a rug over a stack of beer crates, all the while clutching an ice-cold Estrella Galicia. Less afraid and with a more open gaze, he tells me I should go to Al Janiah in the city centre, to see Mohamad and other Palestinians gather in a restaurant that's always busy and forever full of discussion and food. Aiman says he's not a refugee. Mohamad and his son are, and he's there to help them. Mohamad lives in a tower block that has been taken over by homeless people; the bottom five floors are occupied by Brazilians, the top five by refugees. Aiman wears a red and white *hata*, the scarf that became a symbol of Palestine thanks to Yasser Arafat. A regular customer greets him, 'Hey Palestine!', to which Aiman replies: 'Jesus was my cousin!' Aiman has an Israeli passport and can travel wherever he wishes to. He has a social-science degree from Israel, has Muslim relatives in a refugee camp in Lebanon, defines himself as an atheist, and has a Brazilian wife. Later on in the evening, he comes out from behind the till to sit beside me. A Brazilian lady and her granddaughter have opened a family photo album on the table. The lady's parents were Lebanese and she wants someone to read the Arabic captions for her, describing scenes from a wedding in 1947. 'Interesting. So it says here that this girl is a servant, but she's maid of honour,' Aiman tells the lady, whose glasses have steamed up with warm tears. The *saj* has run out and Mohamad uses the hot plate to make coffee; his son tidies the pots away ready to go home.

I live in São Paulo, where I was born and where I've recently been running creative writing classes, one in a public library for teenagers from underprivileged backgrounds. Any kind of creative workshop encourages subjectivity; often the value lies not in what gets written, but in the exercise itself, in the unprecedented examination of your own thoughts that writing entails. One day, two Syrian women in hijabs sat in the corner of the room; they'd come to work on their Portuguese and to integrate into Brazilian society. I gave the students a set of photos as a creative prompt and everyone scribbled abstract musings on the sea and the day-to-day, but the two women, a mother and daughter, spurned fiction to express their appreciation at being so far away from war. They took an objective approach to my instructions. A few months later I speak to Dania, the daughter, and she tells me they're from Jordan, where Syrians are badly treated. From Jordan, her father made contact with Brazil-based Syrians and paid someone to meet them and help formalise their paperwork, and someone else to find lodgings. Dania says life is tough, it's a real struggle to find work. As for the photo of the Syrian boy lying dead on a Turkish beach, she says she's had no contact with Syrians who've travelled by boat, so she saw the coverage in the media just like we did. She thinks she'll be in Brazil for the rest of her life, even get married one day, but others in her family would like to move to other countries, some even want to go back to Syria. She plans to return one day, but just for a visit, once the war is over. As for being a Muslim in Brazil, she says she encounters a general sense of suspicion, albeit not from all Brazilians, whereby her religion is associated with terrorists, people who, Dania says, seek only to ruin Islam's image.

I think it important that I talk to an institution that provides shelter to refugees and the first place that comes to mind is the Our Lady of Peace Church. It has been welcoming immigrants to São Paulo since the mass arrival of Italians in the nineteenth century, but when the taxi driver drops me off there he says: 'Here you go, the Haitians' church.' The whole neighbourhood is associated with homelessness, slum dwellings, contraband and crack addiction. The church itself is surrounded by a courtyard protected by railings; a Haitian sells green bananas at the gate and holds an umbrella to shelter from the sun. On Wednesdays, hundreds of Africans and Latin Americans gather at the side entrance waiting for the doors to open for a support programme that includes document mediation, cultural adaptation tutorials, medical assistance and overnight lodging, similar to what the Hospedaria dos Imigrantes used to offer. The church welcomes reporters and researchers, provided they book ahead, and I'm joined by nine students, including a photographer and a film-maker seeking inspiring human stories.

We're immediately reminded that this is not an NGO, but a support service provided by a Catholic church. The mission was founded by João Batista Scalabrini, an Italian clergyman concerned about the plight of workers moving abroad in what was a major period of Italian migration in the late nineteenth century. Having heard stories of compatriots dying overseas without a priest, he founded a missionary congregation based on charismata for immigrants. These days, the São Paulo mission attends to people from thirty-three different countries, including domestic migrants – the city's transient population, people who work at sea and spend long periods away from their families or who travel to other regions for seasonal work – as well as refugees and exiles. Besides the parish church there is a refuge, which housed Vietnamese and Korean refugees in the seventies, for example, and now welcomes Haitians, Angolans, Nigerians and Latin Americans: Bolivians, Peruvians, Paraguayans and Chileans, for the most part. There are Masses said in Spanish for the Latin Americans and altars for the Virgin of Guadalupe (Mexico), the Virgin of Caacupé (Paraguay), the Virgin of Chiquinquirá (Colombia), the Virgin of Carmen (Chile), the Virgin of Los Treinta y Tres (Uruguay) and the Virgin of Copacabana (Bolivia). Since 2012, there have also been masses for Haitians, 80 per cent of whom are evangelicals. Thus the Catholic community shares its church with non-catechists, atheists, agnostics and Muslims. The refuge is clean and well-ventilated. Two children, an albino boy and his younger sister, chase around our legs, their clothes tatty through play or lack of a change of outfit. It is a place of fluctuating guests; one in, one out; 110 beds to spend the night in, then out to seek work and alternative lodgings during the day. The refugees sit in the sun in the courtyard, always as a group, and it is a long time before I hear a ripple of laughter. Due to social conflicts, the refuge typically takes in a lot of pregnant women and mothers with children, and although there is no fixed period of stay, on average they get two months' board. The church gives talks in English, French and Spanish about how to fit in culturally, about local labour laws and Brazilian customs. It also performs mediation work between potential employers and potential employees, for just as the refugees are advised on integration, so, too, do the businessmen need orientating. There have been cases in which employers have bypassed the mediation process and recruited Haitians directly from the church courtyard, something the mission condemns. Once contracts have been signed, social assistants go to vet the working environment, often encountering slave-like conditions, especially when it comes to garment manufacturing. For a while now, Haitians have ceased to be recruited and some have even begun to return home. Our guide instructs us not to take photos, telling us about a camera crew that upset an Angolan who didn't want his family to see him in such a sorry state, and reminding us to be sensitive to the fact that trafficked people may not wish to be exposed.

As we come to the end of our supervised tour, the guide tells us that a refugee is unlikely to end up sleeping rough, that they don't fit in well at the homeless hostels, which are set up for a different profile of people, and so many end up in slums or squats. An image comes to mind that seems to explain the ethos of the church's involvement – the refugee as Jesus on his pilgrimage. 'Yes, that's it,' says the guide, and he tells me to read Matthew 25, The Judgement of the Nations:

> When saw we thee a stranger, and took thee in? Or naked, and clothed thee?
>
> Or when saw we thee sick, or in prison, and came unto thee?
>
> And the King shall answer and say unto them, Verily I say unto you, Inasmuch as ye have done it unto one of the least of these my brethren, ye have done it unto me.

MATTHEW 25:38–40

I first heard about Luambo Pitchou, a refugee from the Democratic Republic of Congo (DR Congo), in my neighbourhood record shop. I made contact via Facebook and he suggested we meet in Lapeju, a city-centre bar. The bar is actually a house. The owner used to invite friends over for a drink and one day threw the doors open to the public. Now he hosts alternative events like the ones Pitchou organises to introduce refugees, their work and culture, to Paulistanos. The events feature gastronomy, music, handicrafts and talks. I arrive early and try on the head-wraps a Senegalese couple are selling. They are both Muslim, though her clothing in no way suggests her religion. Pitchou arrives seeming a little anxious. He says he will come and talk to me as soon as he has resolved a few issues, details that I, as a punter, am totally oblivious to. I sit at the bar and get chatting to the Brazilian barman, telling him about the piece I'm researching. His name is Richard and he offers to contribute, for he lives near the 'Haitians' church'

69

and witnessed their dramatic arrival in 2015, when more than four hundred Haitians arrived after an eighty-hour bus journey from Acre state, where the governor had dispatched them to São Paulo without giving the São Paulo authorities more than a moment's notice. The Lapeju barman continues: 'Tião Viana [the governor of Acre] just stuck everyone on a bus, without so much as a toilet, and sent them packing, off to São Paulo, where they were dropped off at the church door. Some of them told me they'd paid three thousand dollars to a coyote to get to Brazil. They're very reserved and most of them just want to go home.' Their journey, according to reports on several news sites, began by bus, going from Port-au-Prince, Haiti, to Santo Domingo, capital of the Dominican Republic, from where they flew to Panama, to continue via bus or plane to Ecuador, and on to Peru, where they made for the Brazilian border, finally reaching Assis Brasil, a small frontier town in Acre state.

When Pitchou returns I ask him about the events he organises and the African refugee situation in general. Pitchou was a lawyer in the DR Congo and now works as a forklift-truck driver. He launched these events because he knew a lot of refugees made handicrafts or were musicians and cooks, but had nowhere to showcase their talents. His goal is to bring about cultural exchange through food, music and debate. He's been in São Paulo for six years. He didn't chose to come to Brazil, but it is where he ended up and he has never left. He's the chief coordinator of GRIST (Homeless Refugees and Immigrants Group, *Grupo dos Refugiados e Imigrantes Sem Teto* in Portuguese), which provides housing support to new arrivals. Refugees are initially sent to the local authority's 340-bed refugee centre, but according to ACNUR (*Alto Comissariado das Nações Unidas para os Refugiados*, known as UNHCR in English), there are some eight thousand refugees in São Paulo, and even that figure only accounts for the official ones. All refugees must register at the refugee centre, but the centre has to maintain a high turn-over and refugees are given very little time to find alternative accommodation. Without speaking Portuguese or having the proper paperwork, they go out to find a bed for the night and end up in squatted buildings so as not to sleep on the streets. Such a scenario encourages slave labour, for unscrupulous businessmen take advantage of the situation by offering jobs to refugees that include board and lodgings but practically no pay for sixteen-hour shifts. Refugees agree to such terms even knowing it is slave labour, just to survive. Pitchou tries to combat immigrant exploitation by making it a matter of collective understanding, and he is inordinately grateful to the MSTC (City Centre Homeless Movement, *Movimento dos Sem Teto do Centro* in Portuguese), a collective that gives refugees a certain freedom by admitting them into their occupied housing movement. Pitchou says that if refugees have any voice at all, it's thanks to the MSTC, and when tackling any accommo-dation problem, the MSTC squats are the first point of call.

Pitcho pauses our conversation; Lapeju is now full of Brazilians, and he turns down the background music (Congolese pop) to give a brief introduction of the food on offer. He says meat is a luxury item in the DR Congo, so few traditional dishes feature animal-based protein. I opt for the *sambusas*, delicious fried pasties stuffed with mushrooms and vegetables, with a glass of pineapple and ginger juice, then banana and almond pudding. There are side plates of spring greens, cabbage, spinach, potatoes and rice. Picking up where he left off, Pitchou says that Congolese people come to Brazil because there are serious problems in the DR Congo; there has been war for twenty years because of coltan, a mineral that is a mixture of columbite and tantalite and a key component in making electronic devices. According to Pitchou, 70 per cent of the world's coltan stocks are found in the DR Congo and six million people have died in the war, yet international news agencies barely ever mention it. Congolese people come to Brazil because of poverty, but it's a poverty that's a strategy of war. Pitchou asks me to imagine a city where women are raped en masse and where rape is used as a weapon to force families to flee their land in terror. 'People are born, raised and nurtured amid war, so what can they do?' Pitchou asks. 'They leave to save their skins,' he says, answering himself. He stresses that people do not leave the DR Congo because Brazil is paradise. It is a nice place, certainly, but that doesn't make it a paradise, the same way the DR Congo is not hell on earth. He feels accepted in São Paulo and gestures at those present, Paulistanos all of them, none of them refugees. Pitchou says refugees must speak for themselves, for they have no representation, indeed the term 'refugee' has become representative precisely because it suggests a lesser citizenship. He says it's especially difficult being an African refugee, you have to wait two years to get your papers, whereas Syrians get theirs much sooner, which makes no sense to him. He doesn't see why war in Syria should be considered any more important than war in the Congo. Pitchou believes the distinction, as made by various institutions and organisations, could end up fostering hatred among refugees, because what, ultimately, are the criteria? Pitchou says that Syrians, for example, already benefit from a support network in São Paulo, they arrive knowing where to go, the same as the Japanese and the Chinese. It's the sort of network that Africans lack and that GRIS is trying to put in place, seeking to avoid conflict by establishing a solid, independent platform that all refugees can use and where they might come together as a collective force.

Still in the city centre, I call in on Adus, an organisation committed to promoting refugee integration. Adus is based on a pedestrianised street near an abandoned hotel that has been entirely taken over as a squat. I wait in the foyer for Erika, a journalist who volunteers at Adus. A Haitian woman is being attended to at reception, all the while feeding a newborn baby that's having some difficulty breathing. The mother tries to curtail the wailing by rocking the child in one arm, rummaging for documents in her bag with the other. From where I'm sitting, I hear her answer the receptionist's questions: 'I speak French, I'm single, I have five children, I'm Christian.'

I must say I've frequently felt uncomfortable researching this piece, be it speaking to the Palestinians or Pitchou or approaching the Haitians in the churchyard. Erika puts my mind at ease somewhat by beginning our conversation by talking about curiosity, explaining that she always welcomes journalists to Adus and is accustomed to mediating between vulnerable refugees and the nature of newspapers and deadlines. Erika instructs colleagues to never ask refugees why they left their own countries. She has been involved with Adus for three years, but readily recalls her own initial sense of curiosity. She asked the first refugee she met what had caused her to come to Brazil; the woman immediately took fright and fled, leaving her children behind. Erika still feels guilty about it, and this guilt resurfaces whenever she hears a volunteer, journalist or visitor ask the killer question. Indeed it's a rule at Adus never to ask. Erika says you can often tell by reading between the lines whether a person was politically engaged, for example if they used to be a lawyer, but you should never enquire directly. She says they deal with a lot of women who have left families behind and she speaks of a Nigerian woman who left her daughters with her mother-in-law but was worried because they were reaching the age of genital mutilation and she wanted to bring them to Brazil. She hadn't the financial resources, so Erika offered to publicise the case and try to raise funds, but the Nigerian woman would not allow her photograph to be used, meaning she was probably illegal and couldn't have brought her daughters over anyway. Erika says there's no way of Adus knowing whether a woman has or hasn't suffered genital mutilation, but she suspects it might even happen here, on Brazilian soil, for it's a cultural convention, perhaps a mother or grandmother knows how to perform mutilations, a granddaughter comes over and is subjected to it, or so Erika speculates. But even with the proper paperwork, how could they have raised the money? Erika doesn't beat about the bush: 'She was Nigerian. If she'd been Syrian, it would all have been dealt with quickly.' She confirms it's much easier for Syrians than Africans, just as Pitchou said.

There are two city-centre streets where the influx of African refugees becomes especially clear after nightfall, when dozens of them gather, close the road off and light a barbecue, conversing in languages such as Lingala and Swahili. According to Erika, this assembly has consolidated over time and is a means of preserving identity, languages and customs. Normally Africans head to the city outskirts to live, where it's easier to rent a property without needing a guarantor or having to pay a deposit, and where there are more black people generally, meaning the new arrivals feel less discriminated against and can tap into mutual support systems. A Congolese refugee told Erika he'd never experienced prejudice before coming to São Paulo, for although there are physical differences between Bantu, Nilotic and Pygmy people in the Congo, they are nevertheless all black. Refugees are always more fragile than volunteers expect. Erika recalls helping a refugee from Sierra Leone. It was night-time, it was raining and the hostels were all closed, so the director decided to put the refugee up in a nearby hotel for the night and see to him in the morning. In the hotel foyer it turned out the man had never been in a lift before; he had to be coaxed inside and shown how to press the numbered buttons. It is for reasons such as these that Adus offers an IT course, because refugees nowadays have to be digitally literate, to know how to start computers, open Word documents, use email accounts.

Erika says she's got used to the cultural differences over time. For example, she gives Portuguese classes in a mosque and has learned to greet Muslims without being overly effusive. She tries to be non-judgemental, no matter how hard it might be, especially in cases of domestic violence, something Adus is highly sensitive to but seeks to tackle by teaching rather than imposing rules. They speak to the women, but mostly to their husbands. Erika recalls a forum designed to help refugees understand the Brazilian legal system where someone asked: 'If my wife cheats on me, can I kill her?' Erika introduced the man to the 'Maria da Penha' law, established in 2006 to legislate against violence towards women. Although the murder rate for women is on the decline in São Paulo, 106,093 women were nevertheless killed in Brazil between 1980 and 2013. Erika says children often reveal that fathers beat mothers, but the volunteers are powerless to intervene because the women refuse to report it. In many cases, only the husband will have the proper paperwork, so if a woman decides to leave him, she'll likely end up homeless. Female refugees tend to suffer more anyway, Erika says, for they're easier to identify. Brazilians are visibly a very multi-ethnic people due to extensive miscegenation, to the point that Brazilian passports are highly prized on the black market because almost anyone could have been born in Brazil. In the case of a male Arab refugee, he might pass as second-generation Lebanese, but a female Muslim is immediately recognisable because of her hijab. It's the same thing with African men, who blend in perfectly unless they're heard speaking a foreign language, but women stand out due to their fabrics, necklaces and head-wraps.

When the image of the dead Syrian boy on the beach caused a media storm, Adus became inundated with requests for interviews and offers of donation. The problem was that the phone would often ring with people pledging specifically to help Syrian families. Erika would inform callers that Adus helped all kinds of refugees, not just Syrians. If they wished to donate exclusively to Syrians they would have to do so through a mosque, but Adus made no such distinctions. She was able to talk most people round by contextualising the wars in Syria and the DR Congo, but the callers' obvious prejudice means volunteers have to work hard educating against it. As for prejudices and integration within the refugee community, Erika notes that, even at the mosque, where people share the same religion, there is practically no spontaneous mixing. She says Syrians, Palestinians, Africans and Bengalis greet each other when they go to pray, but they don't mingle, she's heard it said that at functions there will be an Arab table, an African table, a Haitian table and so on, and that even among Africans there is very little intermingling. In the case of the

Haitians, it's arguably because they've suffered so much. Erika recalls the horrific incident of a Brazilian man opening fire on them with a shotgun outside the 'Haitians' church', shouting for them to go back to Haiti, so it's understandable that they choose to keep themselves to themselves and don't like giving interviews. They live a life analogous to having been granted asylum, for they have been afforded humanitarian visas because of the earthquake. At the height of their arrival at the mission, the priest erected a giant shed and filled it with mattresses, so that nobody would have to sleep on the street. But there have since been reports of brawls in which people have tried to steal the Haitians' passports, precisely in order to access humanitarian visas.

A new law was passed in Brazil to facilitate the arrival of Syrians and others fleeing war in Syria. CONARE (National Council for Refugees, *Comitê Nacional para os Refugiados* in Portuguese), for which the Federal Police is responsible, took nine months to issue the visas, after the agreement itself had been finalised in just three months. However, according to Erika, and just as Pitchou said, the Congolese have suffered civil war for twenty years and it takes two to three years for their visas to be processed. 'Why such a difference?' Erika wonders. The Congolese are forced to make do with a flimsy piece of paper, often written by hand, that in no way resembles an official document. This scrap of paper lacks all credibility, making it hard for them to open bank accounts, enrol at schools or sign up for public healthcare. So unconvincing is it as a document that NGOs and projects like the mission have to get their legal departments to confirm the validity of the piece of paper issued by CONARE. Erika reminds me that Brazil is rarely a refugee's first-choice country. The majority want to go to Europe, the USA or Canada. In São Paulo, there are doctors stitching trouser hems in Brás, clinical engineers operating *kibbe* deep-fat fryers, Congolese lawyers cleaning toilets. Many of them suffer from depression, to which end Adus employs a psychologist fluent in English, French and Arabic on a daily basis. The organisation plans to set up an art therapy project for children, having seen them hide beneath tables during firework displays for the 2014 World Cup, thinking bombs were falling. There are children who don't talk, others who are forever jittery or aggressive, some who still use nappies, others who bite tables, and those who are overly mature for their age.

Erika bids me farewell by saying that when walking through the heart of Brás you can hear the whole world on a single street – Africans selling fabrics in a mixture of French and Lingala, Chinese and Korean further down, Arabic at the corner, a world tour.

Brazil is not an easy country even for Brazilians; it was the last place on earth to abolish slavery, in 1888, although the exploitation of immigrants by some businessmen means slavery is really still with us. In São Paulo, unlike other state capitals, it is taken as given that the majority of people don't have roots here. If they don't have a foreign background, they'll likely be from another state, and most will be planning to set themselves up financially before heading back to the south, the north, the north-east. It's a population that sees itself as fleeting, but which ends up entangled in the tentacles of the great *Hallucinated City*. The whole region was first opened up by Bandeirantes, violent men who went on expeditions into the bush to hunt down indigenous people and their riches, men who are today honoured in name by the roads that link the state capital to the interior and coastline. Violence is not something new, it is a burden we bear, one that does not correspond to a carnivalesque people, or perhaps justifies it: we parade and party to cope with the ordeal. In his 'Anthropophagous Manifesto', Oswald de Andrade wrote that joy is 'casting out nines'. That it's not the strongest who survive, but the most adaptable. We're getting there.

SUDANESE SOUTHERNERS

UPROOTED AND DISPERSED

STELLA GAITANO

Translated from the Arabic by Jonathan Wright

STELLA GAITANO was born in Khartoum, Sudan in 1979 and studied Pharmacy at the University of Khartoum. Her short story 'A Lake the Size of a Papaya Fruit' won first prize in the competition 'Creative Writing from the Sudans' (2003). She writes in Arabic and has two full-length short story collections, *Zuhur Zabila* [Wilted Flowers] (2004) and *al-'Aouda* [The Homecoming] (2015). Stella won the Professor Ali El-Mek Award, part of a competition organised by the French Cultural Center in cooperation with the *Al-Ayyam* newspaper in 2001 and 2004.

JONATHAN WRIGHT was a journalist with Reuters for almost thirty years, mostly in the Middle East. For the past ten years he has been translating Arabic literature, mainly contemporary fiction, including works by Youssef Ziedan, Hassan Blassim, Amjad Nasser, Saud Alsanoussi and Alaa Al Aswany. He studied Arabic at Oxford University.

I'M not quite sure how one describes an entire community having to endure exile and displacement, in all their various guises, for decade after decade. People are said to be 'displaced' when compelled to move because their own government mistreats or persecutes them. They are 'returnees' when, after making great efforts and sacrifices to reach a safe country, their dreams are curtailed. They are 'stateless' when stripped of the nationality of their mother country, after one region decides on independence. They are 'refugees' when their new country shatters their hopes and dreams by descending into a gruelling civil war, for no good reason, forcing them to walk back dejectedly from whence they came. The borders seem to move back and forth, but the people end up in the same old places: the same camps, the same miserable conditions and the same poverty.

South Sudanese who have taken refuge in Sudan are in a situation unlike that of refugees anywhere else in the world, and they have been scarred by many painful and sometimes improbable experiences. They feel like second-class citizens in a country where successive governments have mismanaged diversity and failed to achieve balanced development. They became full citizens in their own country after independence, but that was a false start for mostly the same old reasons, or reasons that were even worse than the old ones, when a struggle for power broke out in their new country. They ended up as the victims of politics and returned to the same hellish cycle, whether as abused citizens, the wretchedly displaced, desperate refugees or anxious, stateless people who don't know where they belong.

.   .   .

They called it the second civil war – the war between the government and the southern rebels that lasted from 1983 to 2005. It was a war that had a severe impact on Sudan and its citizens. Close to two million people died, most of them civilians, and some four million people were displaced from the south, abandoning their land and their property to seek safety elsewhere. Most of them were displaced internally, especially to the north. The rest – about six hundred thousand people – dispersed across the countries of eastern Africa and beyond as refugees. The war has been described as the longest civil war in African history.

I'll focus here on those who fled to northern Sudan after their places of origin became battle zones. I well remember how our house became crammed full with the families of displaced relatives – women and children, generally without fathers or sources of income. Then camps for displaced people started to form on the edges of northern towns – camps with names such as Kartoun Kassala ('Cardboard Kassala'), a reference to the fact that all the houses were built of cardboard and sacking, or Jabarouna ('They Forced Us'), a reference to the fact that the residents had been forced to live in these areas, in environments that were alien to them and their culture, in houses that hardly provided shelter, so flimsy they neither shielded them from the sun nor protected them from the rain.

Thousands of families lived in unpleasant close proximity, though the overcrowding arguably gave them a sense of security, despite the difficulties they faced meeting their basic needs. Most Sudanese southerners of my generation were born in places such as these, places identical in every detail, an environment marked by poverty, want, disease and the false hope that we would be going back to the beautiful green south where everything was plentiful, to swathes of land that were all ours, with many head of livestock and fertile fields for farming. There we would live in dignity, growing and harvesting our own food. Displaced people endured this situation for decades because the war did not end. In the meantime, more people were moving north. Some of them adapted to the new environment and made a fresh start, while others preferred to hang on to the dream of going home as soon as possible and went through regular cycles of poverty, ignorance, disease and transitory housing. This gave rise to more poor families that were unable to manage their own lives, and many social diseases appeared – alcoholism, street children, violence, social injustice – although many families did weather the storms and produce positive offspring who were influential in their societies. Others sought dangerous ways to emigrate, some disappearing and some reappearing years later, after losing contact with their families.

Peace between the south and the Sudanese government came about through a long process mediated by international and regional efforts. It culminated in the Comprehensive Peace Agreement of 2005, which came as a welcome relief to all Sudanese, especially the southerners. One of the most important articles in the agreement gave the people of south Sudan the right to self-determination.

The peace agreement's implementation was marred by many flaws and faced a series of obstacles that shook people's belief that it could survive and succeed. The greatest disaster was when the southerners lost former rebel leader Dr John Garang de Mabior, one of the spiritual fathers and guarantors of the agreement. Garang died in a helicopter crash in the Imatong Mountains – a crash that is still seen as suspicious given that the agreement lost direction after his death. Slogans of self-determination were then raised. The voices of those calling for secession from the north grew so strong that the north decided it would prefer the south to secede, on the grounds that the south was a burden on the north. Thus, hundreds of displaced people began to move south by various means of transport in a process called 'voluntary return'; procedures for a referendum on southern independence began before all aspects of the voluntary return process had been completed and there was much tension in the air, which frightened the Sudanese who were originally from the south. This compelled them to move south in a way that was not properly planned or well-considered, and which would have a heavy effect on their lives and futures. Thousands of families were returning to their birthplaces in the south, a region that had lived through half a century of brutal warfare; war had brought development to a standstill, destroyed what little infrastructure existed and broken people's spirits. It was not a region ready to receive people who had been scattered around the world and neighbouring countries, somewhere that could provide them with a decent life, guarantee work for adults, schools for children and clean water for everyone. Life was so harsh that many people soon decided to migrate back in the opposite direction.

The transitional period for implementing all provisions of the comprehensive peace agreement was set at six years. All southern and northern leaders contributed to the process with unprecedented integrity, maybe with the discreet blessing of the international community. At the height of the referendum process, southerners living in the north became preoccupied with voluntary return programmes, for it seemed a foregone conclusion that the result of the referendum would be in favour of secession. The Sudanese government wanted southerners in the north to vote against secession, and the Sudan People's Liberation Movement in the south was worried that it would happen. In the end, the referendum showed 99 per cent support for southern secession – a percentage that shocked northern Sudan and took the world by surprise. South Sudan became independent on 9 June 2011; that day, anyone associated with the south lost their Sudanese citizenship, even people born and raised in the north. Overnight, close to eight million southerners found themselves stateless and without valid official papers. Even documents relating to work and professional qualifications became invalid. Most of the people affected were in the north; they lost their jobs and their nationality and became foreigners from another country, just like that, without any transitional arrangements. These decisions added noticeably to the flow of southerners on the move. They sold their houses, packed their bags and set off for the south by air, land and riverboat. The town of Kosti, a river port on the White Nile, was packed with people and their belongings. They had come in the expectation that they would reach the south within just a few days. However, other factors were at play in the real world: those few days stretched into years of bitter waiting on quays, in public squares and in ports. They were travelling but not going anywhere, in a state of limbo imposed by the waiting – waiting for something that has still not happened.

As the procedures for repatriation to the south began, intense political, social and economic pressures meant that southerners lost their citizenship rights and were stripped of their Sudanese nationality. The Sudanese government chose a hands-off approach, sending a clear message that the new South Sudan government would have to look after its subjects, despite the fact that the new government was already consumed with managing its own transition from a military to a political movement, from commanding a militia force to managing a state faced with major challenges and deep-rooted problems. The new state's nationals inside Sudan were the least of its concerns at the time, so it ignored the problem and foisted it off on international organisations. On the other hand, the southerners coming home had hoped that things would be better on the other side of the border and cared only about when and how they would reach the Promised Land of South Sudan. But since there were still many issues pending between the north and the south, each of which could lead to all-out conflict between the fragile new state and a legacy state that had many internal problems of its own, almost all the southerners in the north ended up on the street, in camps for people going back to the south, or in public squares in the areas where they had been living. Although these camps had originally been set up for displaced people, over the decades they had become more structured and transformed into residential areas, where most of the southerners had their own homes and some fixed assets and where their children regularly went to schools run by churches or the government. Pressures on the southerners increased after the Sudanese government declared that it was not responsible for anyone from southern Sudan, that it would deny them medical treatment and that they had to return to their own state. This was an excessive and angry reaction to the 99 per cent vote in favour of secession.

Many simple people were frightened. They sold their houses for paltry amounts to estate agents who later sold them to Sudanese citizens at many times the purchase price. Simple people heard rumours that the Sudanese government was going to appropriate their houses or would incite northern citizens against the southerners in order to gain possession of their homes. These rumours bore no resemblance to the truth, but the atmosphere was highly charged and when naivety combined with rumour the inevitable result was that more people decided to return to the south.

The city of Kosti was packed to the brim with families. It was very difficult to predict the repercussions. Rumours and facts mixed together, and the primary beneficiaries of this irresponsible confusion were the Sudan People's Liberation Movement (the South Sudan state) and the National Congress (the Sudanese state), as representatives of authority. The southerners were all under pressure to return to the south without delay. The SPLM wanted its members and southerners to unanimously hail its great victory over the north, and the NC wanted to get rid of people who were a burden and who had sometimes forced it to engage in political and ideological hypocrisy. The NC also wanted to silence the voices that called for diversity and the acceptance of others who differed in religion and culture. As far as the NC was concerned, these were the voices of infidels and secularists, whereas their slogan was an Islamic state ruled by Islamic sharia laws. This had been and still is their overt agenda – that Sudan is an Arab and Islamic state and minorities are petty but irritating sources of conflict. Most of the southerners sold their homes in readiness to move back to the south, willingly or unwillingly. The men were dismissed from their military and civilian jobs. Children were pulled out of schools. They packed up their possessions and put up shelters along the roads in the expectation that the International Organisation for Migration would come and repatriate them to the south. Tens of thousands of families wanted to go back, and yet the south, which had once seemed so close, was now very distant: conceptually, because it had become a different state, and temporally, because they'd entered these makeshift camps in 2011 and the years had rolled by. Such places may change physically or geographically, but they are all places of exile. The housing is temporary and it is hard to obtain daily basics. Year after year, autumn after autumn, they lose many things – patience, dignity, possessions and the sense of a bright future, because many of their children are unable to continue their education. The public squares in these areas become little camps sheltering those who plan to return to the south but have not managed to. The sequence 'displaced–returnee–stateless–refugee' repeats itself, overlaps. They have been stripped of their Sudanese nationality and yet the majority have not been issued identity cards, which need to be renewed every three months. Whenever the northern and southern governments disagree, which happens often, when one of the governments accuses the other of supporting rebel groups, then the Sudanese government issues statements to the effect that citizens of South Sudan need to make sure their official papers are in order, or else…

As mentioned earlier, the process of separation between south and north advanced rapidly towards its final destination, destroying everything in its path. It deliberately skipped many important stages, procedures that would have laid the foundations for a future relationship based on good neighbourliness between the two states and ensured internal stability in both countries. The most significant omission was, in my humble opinion, a process of national reconciliation. I believe such a process would have been an important and useful experience, that it might have helped prevent new conflicts from breaking out, giving rise to more displaced people, more refugees and more illegal migrants crossing the borders seeking safety and the opportunity to start a new life. This is because civil wars in Sudan, new and old ones, all have the same deep-rooted causes: lack of good governance, equitable development or social justice; a failure to provide more scope for participation. Laying old grievances to rest by mutual consent would have aided stability for Sudanese people in the south and the north. But the two parties overseeing the agreement took an unnecessarily finicky approach to its implementation and many aspects of the secession process were left unresolved, such as the division of oil resources, the exact demarcation of the border, the status of Abyei and other disputed areas, and the humanitarian crisis engulfing citizens of the north and south.

Each of these issues was a time bomb that could spark all-out war between the two states, resulting in more displaced people and refugees. One example of the volatility was the attack on the Sudanese town of Heglig by the southerners after the South Sudan government accused Sudan of shelling its territory. This was months after independence. Whenever emotions became inflamed, most northerners rushed to defend their land from enemies who had previously been their brothers. There were many incidents of harassment at a time when tens of thousands of people were stuck in voluntary repatriation stations, in open spaces, on roads and in the port of

Kosti. Steamships were crowded with people and belongings as southerners prepared to say a final farewell to the north after a long wait to depart. But the Sudanese government wished them ill, because South Sudan had occupied Heglig, and all borders were closed between the south and the north, with no crossings by land, river or air. Returning southerners were thus detained in Sudan and trapped in a nightmare of being personae non gratae and yet, at the same time, banned from leaving. A series of ordeals ensued: their possessions remained on the steamers while they were sent back to the camps, with no guarantees of anything: they were simply told to wait.

Two years after independence, South Sudan descended into a war that the freedom fighters of the past could no longer prevent, now that the north was gone, and they were forced to confront disagreements inherited from their time fighting in the bush. This time they fought each other on the streets of Juba among peaceful civilians. A struggle for power between former allies broke out. There were horrific abuses that forced many people to leave, as displaced people or as refugees.

Then the fighting stopped – but only for a while. A peace agreement was implemented, sponsored by the regional Intergovernmental Authority on Development (IGAD) and imposed through threats from the international community, until fighting broke out again. The numerous guarantees had not succeeded. The southern leaders went to war once again, in the same way, and without any reason worthy of mentioning, further adding to the disappointments, defeats and failures suffered by a people whose hopes and dreams merely amounted to being able to live in safety. This was the war that broke the camel's back. Many people decided to leave South Sudan, vowing never to return, and sought asylum in neighbouring countries such as Uganda, Kenya and Sudan.

As successive wars broke out in South Sudan, thousands of people left their homes and most of them moved, as might be expected, to Sudan, the mother country, where the cultural and linguistic environment was well known to the majority, making it easier for them to communicate and interact. Going back to Sudan was the inevitable choice for most people given the geographical proximity. Thousands of people lined up on the southern side of the border with Sudan and this time the government made statements that ostensibly showed magna-nimity and consideration for the historical ties between the south and the north. The government said that it was opening the border to let in the southerners, that they would be safe in their 'mother country', that they would not be treated as foreigners and that they were not refugees but brothers and sisters. These statements came as an unexpected relief to many people, but after a while the southerners discovered that these circumstances imposed a great burden on their lives. The failure to recognise them as refugees was serious because it meant they were forced to fend for themselves in every respect. Most people fleeing the war were women and children, and so mothers were forced into marginal work, such as brewing home-made alcohol, in order to feed their families. Because rents were too high they had to go back into camps, repeating an endless vicious circle.

There is another factor besides war that results in people becoming refugees. The economic collapse in the south, caused by war and low oil prices, has been one of the 'push' factors that makes asylum abroad an attractive option despite the difficulties. Many people are now seeking asylum in Sudan as a first stop on a longer journey, with young people seriously thinking about crossing the seas, defying the waves to reach distant shores and uncertain futures. Will they arrive there safely, or will the salt water swallow them up in silence?

Efon is a mother in her mid-twenties who has been living in a camp for five years or more. She and her family once owned a house. However, after people started going back to the south they sold their house, packed their bags and went to a voluntary repatriation camp. Her mother left for the south and Efon and her children stayed to look after their possessions. Efon has six children in her care, one of them a niece who has lost her mother and her father.

'We've been here for five years,' she said. 'My eldest son was ten years old and now he's a teenager. I've had two children in the camp. My husband lost his job because he's no longer a Sudanese citizen and we couldn't go back to the south. We have a very hard time because we rely on ourselves for everything, although we've lost everything. In order to stay alive, and for our children to continue receiving an education, there had to be a source of income, so I was forced to make beer and sell it to make money to live off. But we run the risk of being arrested by the police whenever we try to smuggle the beer out of the camp to sell it. Then we are imprisoned and fined millions of [Sudanese] pounds that none of us can afford, and then our children lose their sponsor and cannot go to school.

'The new camp that we've moved to is so remote that it's hard for the children to walk to school as they used to. We've had to make an agreement with a bus driver to provide transport for the children in the camp so that they can get to school and back. Each child has to pay six Sudanese pounds [about 24 cents] a day, and I have five children at school, which comes to thirty pounds [about US$1.20] a day, not including breakfast. It's a large amount and we need real help with this. Some organisation came along once and promised to arrange transport for the children. It registered them all, but then it disappeared, like other people who come and then disappear without us seeing any assistance.

'We really don't know how long this situation will last. We feel we have lost our past and our present and we don't have normal lives since everything is an ordeal to get hold of. I'm the one who insists that my children at least continue their education, whatever the circumstances, so that we don't lose our future too. We are hoping that the situation will settle down and we can go back to a normality that we've forgotten.'

A.B., a woman in her mid-forties, has been stuck in a small camp in the middle of the neighbourhood she used to live in, all her attempts to return to the south having failed. She finally lost hope of ever going back when violence broke out there and other people started returning to the north.

'I don't want to die here,' she began. 'I have spent more than a quarter of a century in camps, being driven from one place to another. I have given birth to most of my children here and I haven't been able to establish a reasonable family life. I wasn't able to look after my children properly in such an unstable environment, so I lost them all. I have buried six of my children as young men and women, and some of them had already had children. Two of them committed suicide. One son hanged himself using my dress, leaving three children behind, their mother wandered off and left them to me. One of my daughters poisoned herself and we couldn't save her in time.

She left two children, a boy and a girl, and I've been looking after them besides my own young children. The others died of chronic diseases or from alcoholism.

'I'm a single woman and solely responsible for these children, living in appalling conditions. Sometimes I go out to work in people's houses, washing clothes even on days when it is bitterly cold. Sometimes we walk long distances to the farms to help harvest vegetables. We are paid in whatever vegetables we are picking, some of which we sell and the rest of which we eat. I'm ill now. My joints are very painful. I handed two of the children to an Islamic organisation, which made them convert to Islam and memorise the Qur'an. That organisation is now looking after them. The others are in the nearby school, but I'm exhausted and have completely given up hope that I will be able to raise them to adulthood.

'On top of being worried about this situation, which has already deprived me of my children, the state we are living in is appalling and it's hard to lead a happy life. We are forever afraid and we don't know when it will end and how it will come to pass. Children are drawn to bad habits in adolescence, such as stealing things and harming themselves. I wish we could have reached South Sudan, even if we would have died there. I think death would have been easier than this.'

S.M., a woman in her mid-twenties: 'I've been living in this camp since the south became independent. At the time we had high hopes, but instead we've been stuck here, for what seems like forever. The family has been broken up – some reached the south, some of us are in Egypt and some of us are here. We are all looking for ways to get out to anywhere safe, and looking for a new life instead of this life of wars, displacement and seeking refuge. We want stability. I work in people's houses. I leave the camp early in the morning and come back in the evening. Half my earnings go on transport between the camp and the places where I work since we have to get three different connections to reach the town centres.

'I don't want to make alcohol again because I've spent enough time in jail for brewing it and selling it. Besides, the fines are very high, more than six million [Sudanese pounds], and now we are foreigners here, subject to many pressures and exploitation. The situation is difficult in the camps and we don't know who is responsible for us. There is no assistance from anyone, not even from our government or our embassy. No one has ever come to investigate the situation we're in. Right now it's bitterly cold and there's little food and our houses don't even protect us from the cold. We made them ourselves from basic materials – empty sacks, pieces of wood and bits of corrugated iron. We're not like internationally recognised refugees, because we have no status of any kind. What makes us like other refugees is that we're crammed into camps, but the rest we have to put up with ourselves, on our own.'

There are many different versions, but the story is always the same, with the same sprawling roots: war, no sense of security, governments that expel people, other countries that might be able to but are not prepared to take anyone in – especially when the people in question are weak, in every way, but particularly in terms of education and skills, and when they lack the financial resources to initiate projects that might generate income and benefit the host country. It's hard to break out of the cycle of poverty and want. It is a bitter and painful feeling when you sense that you are a burden and everyone is afraid to give you a helping hand. You feel as if you will have to keep asking for help again and again and it might go on indefinitely and maybe eternally. You feel you are a burdensome and unwelcome guest, because you have a reputation for being antagonistic. After all, you voted 99.9 per cent in favour of secession from the north, and then, less than three years later, you're back again, head hanging low, tail between your legs. You've come back to the same place and the same people, abandoning any last sense of dignity. In the meantime, the prospect of emigrating and finding asylum in preferred countries has shrunk to almost zero.

We are trapped in the snares of blind policies, bad governance and corruption – snares that, if they don't kill you, will kill your children. Even if you manage to survive, you will not be in good health. You will bear on your shoulders and in your heart social and psychological scars that will last much, much longer than the time you spent in the camps. You will look in every direction in search of a compassionate helper. You will put out your hand as far as you can reach to receive something: a roof over your head, bread, water, a blanket to fend off the cold – maybe even a country to live in.

All this violence, these wars, the internal displacements and the flows of refugees, the cruel conditions and the fear of 'the other', show the level of barbarism we humans have sunk to. Doesn't this count as failure? This question I address to the leaders of the world today – to those who sit on the governmental throne of this war-ravaged country, to those who stir up terrorism, and to the wealthy who trade in weapons of destruction. Have they not asked themselves this: Why is the world more violent than it used to be? Why is the world no longer safe for anyone? Why this reversion to primitive barbarism? Why internal wars rather than wars between states? Why has this happened when we are in power? Where have we failed, we rulers of the world today? Why is humanity suffering on our watch? Why do people complain wherever they go? Why this cruelty and this violent oppression?

Just as any displaced person longs to return to his or her birthplace, do refugees not long to return to their own country? Why do we first think of resettling them when they already have a homeland? The only issue is that their homeland is in crisis because of wars, most of which are absurd and benefit only a minority of greedy and perverse people. Millions of dollars are dispensed to host countries to spend on refugees. If only half that money was spent on restoring security, eliminating corruption, laying the foundations for good governance, justice, equality, balanced development and the peaceful, democratic transfer of power in the home countries, would Africans, Asians and Arabs have to cross seas to find those values in other countries? Would European countries have to worry about the thousands of migrants who enter their territory by devious means? Would they be in such frenzied competition to sign intercontinental agreements to control and close borders between countries of transit and receiving countries? Would America need to feel anxious about its national identity?

In fact, we still don't know the consequences of these extraordinary migrations – the emigration of qualified people from countries of the south to countries of the north, from the Third World to the First World – an unfair transaction that strengthens the strong and enfeebles the weak to the point of utter fragility.

Nostalgia for the home country will persist and, in the same way that human rights organisations have emphasised the right to asylum due to governments going to war or oppressing their people, the human rights community must also emphasise and speak more boldly about the right to live in your own country, the right to build your own country, the right to produce and think and be creative. But international agencies merely help us overcome crises. They may help us get rid of the corrupt dictatorships that govern us, that manipulate us, spoil our dreams and force us to seek refuge abroad. But we do not want to sail across the sea to exchange one slow death for another, on the off-chance we might manage to start a new life. We want to be here, in our own country, doing wonderful things and creating a civilisation. We want others to come and visit us. We want to amaze them in the same way we are amazed when we go abroad and lose our identity. Abroad we have to adjust ourselves, like old clothes refitted to suit new cultures and new languages, while our mother tongues fade away, our cultures wither and our various identities die, strangled in the process of adaptation. I fully believe that every human being is important and every culture is important, but I like to compare these emigrations to desertification and erosion processes that eliminate diversity and difference. The ego of the emigrant simply dissolves into 'the other' of the substitute country, because those who live in other people's houses lose their freedoms as human beings. They lose the radiant sense of purpose that comes to them when they're in their own country. They always feel they owe others a favour, and this hangs around their neck like a garland, and they have to bow down to the host people and the host government, even if they disagree with them. Yes, it might be a life full of hopes and dreams and opportunities, but the sense of shortcoming will persist like an itch on the back their hands can't reach. Whenever something goes wrong, even if it is just an isolated incident, their hearts twinge with a mild sense of humiliation.

When we talk about internationalism or universalism, we are serious and we are seeking to achieve carefully chosen things. It's easy to talk about intercontinental global trade, global health and health security, the United Nations and its legally validated resolutions, climate change and the hell of global warming, saving the environment and future generations' rights to resources. Why don't we talk more seriously about world peace and global security, since any security failure in any region can result in a violation that affects other states? Which is generally what happens. Or the security failure imposes a burden on another government. Or people in one country are forced to grudgingly accept people from another country, often for long periods. Then there are the horrors faced by people who are directly affected by the violence in their regions. I continue to advocate the right of every individual to live in peace in their own country, without being forced to emigrate, seek asylum, lose their identity or be subjected to discrimination.

To live in dignity and enjoy full rights that are unimpaired, even if the impairment is subjective and emotional, people must have a country of their own. Dignity is tied to the right to object and oppose. Dignity is tied to effective participation in society, as workers or as artists, and to demands for as few constraints to hopes and aspirations as possible. Can countries of refuge meet all these conditions to provide a dignified life? The more frightening question is this: Can we demand such things? I don't think so. World leaders today, and specifically the leaders of the most powerful and influential countries, can make a difference merely by taking a simple decision: to ensure that people who might otherwise have to emigrate and seek asylum can stay safely in their own countries, to make sea crossings safer and to protect people from the evils of closed borders. No matter what sanctions are imposed, they no longer work. Ordinary people are directly affected by these sanctions, more so than the ruling elite, and are expected to submit to demands so that peace or some other objective can be achieved. I remind myself that it was economic collapse in south Sudan that drove us out, more than it was the wars themselves.

Peace, security, political and economic guarantees and an end to wars driven by vested interests are the demands that many refugees around the world are making. These are the demands of the millions of children for whose sake we want to stop global warming, economise on fresh water and protect the environment, in order to make tomorrow's world sane, possible and habitable.

REFUGEES AND MIGRANTS AT THE NADOR BORDER

NAJAT EL HACHMI

Translated from the Catalan by Peter Bush

NAJAT EL HACHMI was born in Morocco in 1979 and moved to Spain in 1987, where she earned her degree in Arabic Studies from the University of Barcelona. *The Last Patriarch* won the Ramon Llull Prize in 2008 and the Prix Ulysse in 2009 and has been translated into eleven languages; it was published in English by Serpent's Tail, as was *The Body Hunter*. For her latest work *La filla estrangera* [The Foreign Daughter] she received the 2015 BBVA Sant Joan Novel Award and the Ciutat de Barcelona Catalan Fiction Award.

PETER BUSH translated *The Last Patriarch* and *The Body Hunter* by Najat El Hachmi. He is currently working on *Salt Water*, stories by Josep Pla, and *Barcelona Tales*, a selection of stories set in Barcelona by writers from Cervantes to Teresa Solana. *Winds of the Night*, his translation of the sequel to Joan Sales' *Uncertain Glory*, will be out in October 2017.

I was on my way to Casablanca airport in February 2016, being driven by the chauffeur of the institution that had invited me to participate in the city's book fair, when suddenly crowds of people appeared on either side of the motorway waving papers and trying to catch our attention. It was a strange, unexpected incident, the significance of which I didn't immediately grasp. Lots of people ask for things on the streets of Morocco, but usually in urban centres, not on the edge of a busy highway. And I also couldn't work out what they were waving in the air. There were men, women and children. All had sunburnt faces, most were white-skinned, though their cheeks, noses, foreheads and chins displayed that characteristic shadow, the singed tone of people who have been living out in the open and walking long distances. Their inflamed skin was really striking, but it was the expression in their eyes that drew me inexorably to their innermost state. Since seeing them, I've been trying to understand what it was about their gaze that managed to hook me in and break down any resistance my conscience might offer. It was something like this: their eyes challenged us, comfortably ensconced in our cars, and penetrated the hidden recesses of our beings – at least that's what I felt at the time. I lowered the window to see them more clearly, feeling guilty, of course, for my curiosity verged on the voyeuristic. But I couldn't help myself, those eyes sought mine out and wanted me to share in a cruel experience that I'd heard a lot about, via mass media and at a distance, but that I'd never seen up close. Imagination is one thing; I can imagine what they have endured and what their current daily struggles must be, but confronting the idea of something is very different to experiencing it in reality: what we imagine is a measure of what we can tolerate. 'They are refugees,' commented my chauffeur, 'Syrian refugees.' They were waving passports to prove that was what they were: that they had escaped from a war the entire world was aware of. I reflected on how sad it was that in order to gain the sympathy of others they had to first demonstrate that they deserved sympathy, as if the stories of who we are and what has happened to us are not enough; as if being an individual and recounting your misfortunes is not enough to receive a helping hand, even in the most extreme situations. Furthermore, that suspicion should predominate rather than a desire to listen to what the other person is trying to tell us.

I imagined the geographical expanses all those refugees must have crossed and I understood why they'd desperately clung on to the bundle of pages that make up a passport, for it was the only thing that could validate who they were and where they'd come from, the barbarism that had been inflicted on their people. How many borders had they crossed to reach the far west tip of North Africa from Syria? Many countries, many different landscapes, with vastly diverse inhabitants, some of whom will have helped them, others who will not only not have helped, but will have put obstacles in their path. Some of the areas they must have crossed are places of socio-political conflict, whether of simmering tensions, such as Egypt and Tunisia, or openly bellicose, such as Libya. That whole odyssey just to reach Morocco, a country that does not recognise their right to asylum. Which is why most were heading for the northern frontier, the one with southern Europe, as represented by Ceuta and Melilla, two Spanish cities on the North African coast. My mother, who divides her time between the town where we were born, in the Moroccan province of Nador, and the city we grew up in, Vic, close to Barcelona, had been telling me for some time about the refugees coming to the area. 'They crowd the streets,' she told me in 2014. 'They beg and don't realise that local people are themselves struggling to survive.'

I hadn't been back to Morocco for seven years. Or rather, it had been seven years since I'd been back to 'my' Morocco, to the place where I was born. And the last time had been a short visit for a television report, so I'm not sure it counts. I flew in on a low-cost flight, a phenomenon that is a far cry from the long journeys my family used to undertake when we went back to Morocco for the summer. I observed the people in the airport on my flight: men and women of different ages, and some children. Very old men, first-wave emigrants, wearing Tergal trousers and knitted hats, and young women in carefully coordinated clothes taking photos with their smartphones.

It seems very strange to reach Nador in under two hours; if you opt for the overland route, the endless hours spent on the road as you cross the length of the Iberian peninsula make the transition from one world to another more tangible; the shift is more physical. You notice the change in landscape; southern Andalusia already seems very like the arid coast of North Africa. But by plane it all happens in two hours: in the seats where we passengers are packed, there is no physical transition – we go from one place on the map to another with no intermediary stages. It gives a false sense that the two realities aren't so very far apart, which is a complete illusion. Air travel was once the preserve of the rich and so flying back to your home town makes you think you've gone up in the world, though the human landscape is almost the same as on the buses, women with babies, tired old people and modern youngsters. The plane spares all of us what was once the most distressing part of the journey: the border crossing.

I have been obsessed with the border between Nador and Melilla for years. As a young girl and adolescent I spent many hours there, my feet tucked beneath me, curled up in the car, waiting and waiting to enter Morocco, because the officials only allowed you to get through quickly if you gave them 'the price of a coffee'. On the way back, to enter Spain, it was the same thing, painstaking and time-consuming border controls, because anyone coming from the south was suspicious. All frontiers are strange, artificial creations that order, segregate, separate and signal a concrete place where one set of realities is marked out from another; it is an artificial location. Cultures, civilisations, whatever you want to call them, tend to change slowly from one into another, not in the drastic, violent manner of crossing a frontier. This particular border is a case in point. The realities of Nador and Melilla aren't so different. If one looks at economic indicators, GNP, unemployment, etc… it's pretty clear that the Spanish city is more like Nador than it is like Spanish cities on the mainland. Moreover, its human landscape is quite similar, for there are many 'Muslims' – in fact they're Riffians, but they get labelled Muslim – who live in Melilla, be they born and bred locals or immigrants, recent or long-term. Conversely, many of these Tamazight-speaking Melillans look down on their counterparts across the border as belonging to a very different social class.

The border has always been a place where people are classified: those who have Spanish nationality and those who do not, those who have permission to reside in Spain and those who do not; those who are from towns near the border and have a special permit that allows them to enter Melilla, but not to cross the strait; those who have relatives in Europe who have arranged documents for them and can cross and those who do not; those who have money (if you can prove you have a large enough sum in your current account you can get a visa without any hassle to enter Schengen territory) and those who do not.

'They don't know where they've landed,' my mother would say when she saw Syrians on the streets of Nador. What do they expect people to give them, if the locals already live in dire poverty? Obviously, the refugees hadn't come to such a poor area in order to stay, that was never their intention, they had travelled there to be near the border to a territory they could set foot in and claim asylum.

Hardly any Syrian refugees remain in Nador now. When my uncle takes me to his house on the city outskirts, we notice some girls by the entrance to a mosque. They are asking for charity, saying 'help me' to passers-by, and someone has the bright idea of asking them if they're really Syrian or if they're lying. The girls insist repeatedly that they are Syrian, that they're from where they say they're from. Their Arabic is so eastern it ought to be proof enough, but the man persists with his joke, which strikes me as cruel and decidedly unfunny. Their hair is whitened by the sun, their faces bear the same shadow I'd seen in Casablanca and their flip-flops drag along the ground when they play jumping games.

The next morning I take a stroll through the city centre. I find a very different panorama to the one that used to greet me when I'd come here in the summer: it is quiet, there are few people around and the hustle and bustle I remember is nowhere to be seen; the place seems to be operating at half-speed. Even the markets are very quiet. It's not that people have left, just that we, the children of immigrants, only know Nador in the summer, when it's thronging with all the families who live abroad and come back for the holidays. We represent an entire social class, the immigrant class, they call us 'the people from abroad'; there must be tens of thousands of us who return every year to visit our place of birth. It is not for nothing that the Rif region has experienced this phenomenon so intensely. Every family has someone who lives abroad; entire families have departed. It is a region that has been punished for decades by drought, exploited by the Spanish protectorate before independence and then deliberately abandoned by Hassan II's regime because of the supposedly rebellious spirit of its people. Migration is part and parcel of the history of every family: first they went to cities in Morocco, then to Algeria and finally to countries in Europe. Spain is a relatively recent destination for emigrants. So every summer you see the streets of Nador fill up with the people who left, with their children and grandchildren, turning everything upside down, inflating prices and altogether disrupting the tranquil daily life I now see here out of season.

But I keep on walking and I don't see any refugees – I really don't. I can't find the scene my mother has been depicting anywhere.

Before I set out on this trip, an acquaintance who lives in France had advised me to speak to a human rights organisation. I made an appointment with Omar Naji, the general secretary of the AMDH, the Moroccan Association for Human Rights (*Association marocaine des droits humains* in French). Their headquarters is in the Lardri Chaik district. Nador's coastal road has been developed; you can see that a lot of money has been spent on the corniche opposite the Mar Chica. They have even built a Mercure Hotel. Clearly the Moroccan government wants to invest in the area and make it attractive to tourists. However, as we walk into the city, the landscape changes radically. The association is based in a poor area with unmade roads, two or three-storey houses in bad states of repair and the usual lack of proper rubbish collection. There is a market next to the AMDH's office, fruit and vegetables on wooden carts or on the ground. I wait by the entrance to the building and a tooth-less old lady asks me what I'm looking for. I tell her about the association and she asks me if I need their help. She tries to persuade me that they're of no use, that they talk a lot but do nothing. 'What do you expect them to do?' she asks me. 'They just spend the money they get on the rent.'

Omar tells me that they are in the process of mobilising people, organising demonstrations in every city in Morocco. They are doing this because a fisherman from Alhucemas was recently run over and killed by a lorry that was carrying fish the police had just confiscated from him. This triggered revolts against the impunity of the *Makhzen* (the elite) and bureau-cratic structures of government that seem a throwback to the corruption and despotism of other, darker times. The greatest fear of both the monarchy and the oligarchic minority that rules Morocco is that there might be an uprising in Morocco to resemble those in Tunisia or Egypt. Not for nothing is Morocco one of the few Arab countries that has not had its Spring, something that seems unlikely to happen, for Mohammed VI's country always appears to be on the point of exploding, but never does.

When I ask Omar about the Syrians, he first tells me that Morocco rarely recognises anyone's right to asylum because that would entail having to assume responsibility for refugees.

He reckons that in 2015 there were almost five thousand people in the frontier town of Beni Ansar, all hoping to enter Spain, and now there are none. There were also Iraqis, Palestinians and Yemenis. 'So where are they?' I ask. 'Ah, that's the big question,' he replies, as if he is about to reveal some key information. Spain has established an asylum office, but it's on the other side of the border, inside Spain. Refugees can see it, but can't get access to it, because you have to actually be inside the country to request asylum. The frontier is becoming increasingly impenetrable. It used to be just the Spanish fence that would be built higher and higher over the years. They even put spikes along the top, lethal razor blades to dissuade people from trying to climb over it. There are security cameras and there's constant surveillance. But now Morocco has installed its own fence, making it well-nigh impossible to reach European soil from here.

I remember my grandfather used to go to Melilla to shop, with his *carte nationale*, with no need for a passport, and that people living in Tangiers could go and spend the weekend in southern Andalusia. A bilateral agreement existed between the two countries, which was logical enough, given their geographical proximity. But one day all that changed. Schengen arrived, Spain became European and decided it was quite different to Morocco. Restrictions were imposed that we put up with as if they had existed forever. Although we were now the ones being classified, we never challenged the legitimacy of the border.

But what had become of the refugees in Nador, where did they go? 'They crossed the border,' says Omar. But how? Seeing as it's impossible… His theory is that there is a people-trafficking network at the frontier that gets the refugees across, as has been reported at various times. Perhaps some people buy Moroccan passports, change the way they look and dress, but five thousand people can't possibly have passed through like that without the complicity of the authorities. They pay between 350 and 1,200 euros to get in, 'just imagine what that means'. Not long ago, a policewoman had apparently been arrested for being involved in people trafficking. That many people could not have crossed the frontier without the help of those in charge of border checks.

As we drove away from El Aroui airport, we saw some black women begging; they were carrying small children on their backs and older children walked by their side. The most common image of the frontier in the Spanish media relates to the occasional attempts made by sub-Saharan immigrants to jump over the fence. When referring to these incidents, television channels and daily papers use language that is far from neutral: 'jumping the fence' is often coupled with 'storm', 'en masse', 'pre-meditated', 'avalanche', 'hordes', etc… a language that unambiguously communicates the peril supposedly represented by these foreigners and naturally gives the impression that our territory is securely protected and that the people governing us know how to safeguard us from 'the other'. The well-honed distinction between refugees and immigrants is one of the incongruities inherent in European public opinion on these issues. The fact is, among the many sub-Saharans who do manage to 'jump' the fence, some are from countries at war, wars that don't receive the same prominence as the war in Syria, because they are old, chronic and, probably, because they take place in Africa. Once again, the frontier establishes categories between one group of people and another. I was surprised not to see more sub-Saharans on the streets of Nador, apart from the women we saw begging. I asked Omar and he told me they were on Mount Gurugu, the mountain nearest to the city. They live in camps, of which he has counted five; camps in a deplorable state, with plastic tents. The sub-Saharans are often brutally beaten by the police who drive up to the mountain to dismantle the tents. 'Nador is the only city in Morocco where there are no black people on the streets, they hide because if the police find them, they transport them a long way away into the interior of the country.'

Before starting out I had phoned Father Estevan Velázquez, as I knew he worked in Nador helping refugees and immigrants. I had been planning to meet him in Nador, but he had been away for some months and the nuns who made up his team were busy that weekend with the visit of a bishop. I asked him why he wasn't in Morocco, and if it was true, as some news reports claimed, that he had been expelled. 'Not exactly expelled,' he replied, 'but they've banned me from returning, which more or less amounts to the same thing.' He tells me that what he used to do, and what the nuns continue to do, was simply to care for immigrants, especially the sub-Saharans living in dreadful conditions on the mountain. They aren't only on Gurugu, but also in Serwan, where they hope to get out on a flatboat. There are camps for women, who he suspects are victims of the slave trade. They also provide medical care for people beaten by the police and they often come across people with broken bones. Some people have even died. Quite a number of the women become pregnant, and they take them to the hospital to give birth. 'Fortunately,' he tells me, 'Moroccan hospitals look after them without creating problems, but, of course, patients have to pay for their medications, and we try to take care of that.'

When we talk about the fence, he says that at present it is impossible to climb over and that immigrants are trying to cross the sea from Al Hoceima in order to reach Almeria or Motril.

As for the local reaction to immigrants, he says that there is a bit of everything: some people try to help, but many others are afraid of approaching them for fear of suffering police repression. And one must never forget the racism that exists in Morocco. In any case it is much more difficult for a sub-Saharan than for a Syrian. Syrians can pass by unnoticed among Moroccans, but black people can't hide the colour of their skin, a colour that means they must endure a specific kind of brutality. I think of the sub-Saharans I have known in Barcelona, long-time acquaintances, and how when I first told them that I was born in Morocco they would say, 'I spent a long time in your country and I was glad to do so,' hoping we shared a bond by having experienced the same landscapes.

State and commercial television channels in my aunt and uncle's house focus on just two topics during the day: the climate change convention in Marrakesh and Mohamed VI's visit to Senegal, where he is welcomed with every honour. Inevitably I contrast the two realities: black people being treated like animals near to where I'm staying, and the monarch who is so clean, so well-dressed and well-fed, shaking hands with other black people who are likewise clean, well-dressed and well-fed.

I don't want to leave without visiting the frontier, without seeing it afresh, this time from the perspective of someone who won't be crossing over. I take a taxi from Nador, sharing it with three women who keep sliding their bejewelled fingers over the screens of their mobile phones. Two men pile into the front seat. The ancient Mercedes make me feel that nothing has changed in Morocco, with the little handle you have to ask the driver for in order to wind down the window. However, the main roads are smoother, better tarmacked, and the whole coast seems like it is about to change radically. Before reaching Beni Ansar, I discover they've built nothing less than a luxury residential complex and golf course. When I reach the Beni Ansar checkpoint, I find it hard to believe how quiet it is, that there are so few cars waiting to cross. It is a Friday in November. Seen from here, the frontier doesn't seem loaded with connotations, doesn't seem enshrined in the world's inequalities. The weather is fine and everything is calm; there is nothing to suggest that it is, in fact, a place where the violence of the wider world might suddenly erupt. But you only have to look up once you're past the buildings near the border checkpoint to see the sturdy, high-wire fence and the security cameras that protect Europe. Around the checkpoint, on the Moroccan side, the narrow funnel-like stretch of land is horrendous. There are beggars, street children sniffing glue, old women in a dreadful state, and youngsters aged before their time. A second-hand market sells all manner of filthy, old items displayed on wooden tables or spread out on the ground. Here the detritus from the world on the other side is recycled, a world that is so near and yet so out of reach.

WHERE SHOULD THE HAZARAS GO?

MOHAMMED HANIF

MOHAMMED HANIF was born in Okara, Pakistan in 1965. His debut novel *A Case of Exploding Mangoes* (2008) was longlisted for the Man Booker Prize and the Guardian First Book Award and won the Commonwealth Writers' Prize. His second novel, *Our Lady of Alice Bhatti* (2011), was nominated for the Wellcome Trust Book Prize and the DSC Prize for South Asian Literature. Now living in Karachi, Hanif is a columnist for the *New York Times International Edition* and BBC Urdu. He has written the libretto for the forthcoming opera *Bhutto*.

2012 was a bad year for the Hazara community in southern Pakistan. It had been devastated by a series of targeted killings and suicide attacks. Even its protectors-in-training weren't safe. Police cadets belonging to the Hazara community and mid-ranking police officers had been assassinated. That year I interviewed a leader of the ethnic Hazara Shia community in Quetta about the Hazaras' future prospects. Abdul Qayyam Changezi was weary of attending funerals of loved ones. The Hazara community concentrated in a district of Quetta is small, so chances are high that whenever someone gets killed one either knows the deceased or a member of their family. Changezi had come up with a desperate solution to save his people. 'It's quite obvious that the government and security agencies are either not interested in protecting us, or are incapable of doing so,' he said in measured sentences, without anger, as if trying to argue his way out of a mass murder. 'The government should sell everything we own. Our houses, businesses, the furniture in our houses, pots and pans – every single thing. With the proceeds they should buy a large ship, put all of us on it, and push it out into the open sea. Surely there is a country somewhere out there in the world that will have us.'

The ship of Changezi's imagination already existed, and had been transporting human cargo across the rough sea between Indonesia and Australia. Since 2008, when attacks against the Hazara community increased, the Hazaras had been selling up their houses and businesses to go in search of that mythical ship. Many ended up in Malaysia or Indonesia, where they could pay four to six thousand dollars to get on a boat that would take them to Australia and New Zealand, for instance. At the end of a journey that lasted fifty to sixty hours, in the words of one Hazara who made more than six attempts, you either reached the Promised Land or ended up as fish fodder.

Worse was yet to come.

If the Hazaras thought that 2012 was an atrocious year, the year that followed was truly the stuff of nightmares: Hazaras were killed in targeted attacks, their places of worship became death traps, and community elders were systematically eliminated. 2013 was the year of mass murder: in the first two months, two huge explosions killed more than two hundred people and injured thousands. The brutality of these mass killings was only matched by the cruel and half-hearted response of the Pakistani state.

In February 2013, the Hazaras refused to bury hundreds of their dead. In the bitter cold nights of winter they sat on the streets by the coffins of family members and friends, demanding justice, demanding protection. Protests were also held across the country and roads were blocked in major cities. The Pakistani government made vague promises to provide protection, thus persuading the community to hold funerals and bury their dead. But during these protests one thing became clear: the Hazaras were on their own. The only people who turned up at the protests in solidarity were other non-Hazara members of the Shia community. Some politicians and social activists also put in an appearance, but the level of indifference was as brutal as the bloodbath itself. For most Pakistanis living in the big cities where the protests took place, Hazaras were merely a nuisance, disrupting traffic and causing delays in their daily commute.

This was the same argument their killers used to target them. It seemed that the whole country was a silent spectator – if not a cheerleader – to this ongoing atrocity.

The exodus began once it became clear that the killing of Hazaras in Pakistan would not end any time soon – and that the very people tasked with protecting all citizens were helping the killers. Some Hazaras moved to other parts of the country. But the Hazaras' cursed fate is in their face: being of Central Asian descent, their features make them instantly recognisable in any part of Pakistan, and they have historically been targeted in Afghanistan and Pakistan due to their ethnicity. Human rights activists disagree as to whether the Hazara genocide is ethnic or sectarian. Law enforcers surmise that if the Hazaras didn't look so different maybe they would be spared. However, this is not strictly true. Many Hazaras from mixed marriages blend in and yet are still targeted.

The Hazaras' killers even tracked them down in Karachi and killed them. Being Hazara in Pakistan put a target on your back. Death would find you – in a bomb blast, or when a bullet hit you in the back of your head. It made no difference if you worked for the police or a security agency, if you were an Olympian boxer or a famous TV actor – even if you were a much-loved schoolteacher: every Hazara had an arbitrary death sentence hanging over them.

Businessmen closed their shops and stayed home. Government employees were told not to turn up for work and reassured that they would keep getting their salaries. University students stopped going to classes and started hanging around their neighbourhoods. Those lucky enough to be able to sell their houses and businesses ended up in Malaysia and Indonesia, hoping to make it to Australia.

I met Haji Shabbir on the outskirts of Bogor, Indonesia, a hub for Hazara refugees from Pakistan, thousands of whom have been stranded here for three to four years, hoping to get asylum in a Western country. Haji Shabbir almost got lucky. 'We got on the boat. It travelled for about forty hours and then the engine developed a problem. The boat owners had given us a satellite phone, so we called the rescue. They brought us back to Jakarta and detained us in a hotel.' During the night they all escaped. Either the Indonesian police had no interest in keeping them or a bribe exchanged hands. Another attempt by boat was aborted after about sixteen hours. 'Another time, I was supposed to get on a boat, but then I got stuck in traffic and the boat left without me. All in all, I've tried six times. Four years later I'm still here.'

While Hazaras were pouring out of Pakistan to board the mythical ship promising to take them to safety, the Australian government changed its immigration policy. It announced that it would no longer accept refugees arriving by boat and that their cases would be processed offshore. The Australian government took out advertisements in several different languages in Pakistani newspapers and internet portals warning refugees not to attempt the boat journey. To prove that they were serious, they deported vulnerable individuals and minors who arrived by boat.

Outside Jakarta, the town of Bogor and surrounding areas have become a kind of purgatory for Hazara refugees. All they can talk about is the status of their asylum claim, even though there is little to say as most of them have no idea what stage their case has reached. They can make a counselling appointment with one of the UN officials, where they are always told the same thing: 'We are waiting, you should also wait.'

This waiting game can tire some people out. After spending three and a half years in Bogor, Haji Shabbir decided he had waited long enough. 'If I have to die, I might as well go back to Quetta and face my fate,' he says. He contacted the UN representatives and told them that he was withdrawing his asylum application. 'If you choose to go back, the UN pays for your return ticket. I told my family and they said, "Muharram is coming and people are trying to escape from Quetta. What kind of an unlucky man are you that you are returning to Quetta!"' Haji Shabbir stuck to his decision. Then in the middle of Muharram, when the security in Quetta is as tight as it can get, four Hazara women were shot dead while travelling in a bus. Shabbir cancelled his ticket and decided to stay on as a refugee.

What do Pakistan's security agencies do when the Hazaras are targeted? In Bogor I met Mama, a refugee who has been waiting for his fate to be decided for the past three and a half years. He is a former security official from Quetta, who insists on remaining anonymous and asks to be referred to as 'Mama'. From within the system, he watched carnage after carnage unfold and felt utterly powerless. Mama joined the Frontier Constabulary (FC) as a computer operator, where he served for four years. Later his duties included managing the media for the paramilitary force that, along with the police and army, was tasked with maintaining law and order in Quetta city as well as the entire province of Balochistan. 'The FC probably has had as many people killed as Hazara murders have been committed,' says Mama. 'We were totally helpless. Every time any Hazaras got killed, the FC went after suspected Baloch insurgents rather than targeting the actual culprits.' He was part of many meetings and raids that followed major incidents against the Hazaras. 'In these meetings it was often said that the Hazaras were rioting again, rather than discussing how to protect them. After every major incident, we raided villages and rounded up dozens of Baloch youths who clearly had no hand in these attacks. It became a vicious circle. First, the Hazaras would be targeted, following which Baloch communities were raided. Even when they managed to arrest actual suspects, they were handed over to the anti-terrorist force, who held them in lock-ups inside the military cantonment, from where they managed to escape.' Like Mama, many Hazara refugees and independent journalists believe there's a nexus between Pakistan's powerful intelligence agencies and the sectarian militias accused of Hazara killings. A senior clerk in the Special Branch, a civilian intelligence agency, who left his job to seek asylum after his police officer cousins were shot dead, witnessed this complicity first-hand. 'We chased after two terrorists on a motorbike after a targeted attack in Quetta. They drove right through the cantonment gate and disappeared. We told the military personnel that two terrorists had just entered their area and that we were chasing them. We were asked for our identity cards and then told in no uncertain terms to turn around and to never mention the incident to anyone.'

Frontier Constabulary veteran Mama believes that ordinary soldiers have nothing to do with the sectarian attacks. 'A law enforcement agency cannot afford to have a religion. Ordinary soldiers have no clue what's going on around them. It's the intelligence agencies who patronise these sectarian groups. They are out of control. We have no idea whom they are getting their orders from. Obviously they were receiving money from Gulf Arab states wanting to target Shias.'

When Maliha Ali left Pakistan, she was preparing for her O-level exams. For the past three and a half years she and her family have been living outside Bogor in Csurva, and she has no way of taking her exams. Her father, Liaqat Ali Changezi, a former TV actor and documentary producer, decided to leave Quetta with his family after many of his close colleagues had been killed. 'There came a time when the school administration told me to stop sending my kids to school because they were putting the entire school at risk,' says Changezi. He was also asked by the Quetta TV director not to come to work because it was putting all his colleagues in danger.

Having spent more than three and a half years in Bogor waiting for his asylum application to be processed, Changezi feels these are years that have been stolen from his life. His daughter Maliha feels the same. 'They were the most important years of my life: I should be studying, preparing for a future. Instead, we are sitting here waiting for some country to take us in so we can start a new life.'

The biggest challenge Hazara refugees face in Indonesia is that they are not permitted to work and – even worse – are not allowed to go to school. An entire generation of Hazara children is at risk of growing up illiterate. Changezi, with the help of other refugees, has set up a centre where young children can receive elementary education from Hazara volunteers. There are a couple of other such centres that have become community hubs where people can bring their families and seek counselling. Maliha is a volunteer teacher at one such centre. 'Sometimes I think it's ironic that I am at an age where I should be going to school myself, but have become a teacher instead.' When she grows wistful about her time in Quetta, she tries to console herself: 'At least we can play football here. We couldn't do that in Quetta.'

ALL THAT WAS FAMILIAR

ABUBAKAR ADAM IBRAHIM

The author and journalist ABUBAKAR ADAM IBRAHIM was born in Jos, Nigeria, in 1979 and published his literary debut in 2012, a volume of short stories called *The Whispering Trees*. The volume's title story made it to the shortlist of the Caine Prize for African Writing. His first novel, *Season of Crimson Blossoms*, was published in 2015 and won the NLNG Nigeria Prize for Literature in 2016, one of the world's richest literary awards.

EXACTLY twenty-four hours after I'd left Maiduguri, in Borno State, north-eastern Nigeria, the city where Boko Haram first sprung from, hundreds of shabbily dressed people poured onto the windswept streets demanding food.

A friend I'd met during my visit to the ancient capital drew my attention to the news on Facebook. As events unfolded, I followed the story from my home in Abuja, five hundred miles south of the troubled region.

The protesters were internally displaced persons (or IDPs) who, driven by hunger and desperation, had taken to the streets to protest neglect. It was easy for me to visualise how, with what little energy they had left in their bodies, they'd trudged onto the Maiduguri–Kano Road in worn flip-flops, cutting off traffic, waving their fists in the air. In the crowd I imagined the faces of Sa'adatu and Zahra, people I had been with only hours before, people who had survived the indiscriminate bullets of Boko Haram, only to be forced out of their homes and into the relative safety of Maiduguri and its dreary camps for displaced persons.

'Our children are dying,' Bashir Musty, one of the protesters said, 'many are sick as a result of lack of food. All we are saying is we need food to feed our family.' When I read this in newspaper reports, it was the image of Sa'adatu's three hungry children lying on empty sacks on the floor of their shack, wheezing like dying animals, that came to my mind. The image had stuck and it refused to go away.

· · ·

Since Boko Haram began its insurgency in 2011, over two million people have been displaced from their homes in north-eastern Nigeria, northern Cameroon and southern Niger Republic. Only 20 per cent of these individuals are housed in established camps, most of which are in and around Maiduguri. The others have melded into host communities where they live in uncompleted buildings or temporary shacks set up in open fields. Some of them have fled as far south as the nation's capital, Abuja, over five hundred miles away, where there are about thirty camps for IDPs. Some have gone even further south.

Sa'adatu Musa couldn't travel south. Not that she wanted to. She is forty-five, has nine children – the oldest fifteen, the youngest just over a year old – and a husband who she hasn't seen or heard from in ten months.

On the bare floor of her tarpaulin shack, Sa'adatu sat with her legs stretched out before her, cradling her baby, as she shoved a nipple in his mouth. With one hand she brushed the sand out of his hair; with the other she stirred the gruel she was making on an open flame in what was effectively her living room. In one corner there was an array of plastic utensils – buckets, jerrycans and a basin for collecting and storing water – and a stack of old aluminium plates, all clean and dry in a tray on the floor. Next to these were three of Sa'adatu's nine children. They were lying on empty grain sacks spread out on the bare floor, their ribs disturbingly visible. They were skinny and weak and hungry.

'They haven't eaten in days,' Sa'adatu told me as I sat on a stool across the room from her. 'I went out and begged and someone gave me fifty naira. I bought some corn flour with it and I am making this for them.' She stirred the gruel in the old, soot-covered pot.

Multiple reports of displaced persons dying of hunger surfaced in June and July 2016, prompting angry reactions and rebuttals from the Nigerian government and the government of Borno State, where the bulk of the displaced persons are from and where over one and a half million IDPs are currently located. Deaths from hunger may not be prevalent in the many camps around Maiduguri, but they are a reality in camps elsewhere in the state, in Bama, for instance.

In June 2016, photos emerged on social media of government officials re-bagging food meant for IDPs, to sell in the markets. The commandeering of relief materials for IDPs is a common occurrence here. Nutritious milk that UNICEF has designated for starving children regularly turns up in shops, where it sells for about a dollar. Looking at Sa'adatu's children, I imagined how much they could do with that milk – or any milk, for that matter.

This disturbing scene wasn't what I had expected when I arrived at the Bakassi camp. Woolly clouds flecked the blue sky hanging over the red-and-blue aluminium roofs of a fenced-off but unfinished housing estate. The estate is so expansive one would have thought all the displaced persons in Maiduguri could fit into it. The picturesque scenery was disarming, so much so that when the reality beyond the fence hit, it was brutal.

I had arrived in Maiduguri days before. After spending a whole day in the 7th Division Headquarters of the Nigerian Army in Maiduguri, trying to secure authorisation to visit the camps, I was handed a letter on fine quality glossy paper, asking me to return to Abuja and apply through the army headquarters in Nigeria's capital. The whole process would take at least five days. I couldn't understand it. I wanted to write a happy story about the camps, about IDPs finding love and dreaming of returning home. What was the military afraid of? And who on earth would waste such a beautiful piece of paper, glossy and all, just to turn down my request?

A major in the army, smiling effusively as he swivelled in his chair, took the time to explain why they were being so cautious. They had had lots of negative reports from journalists; and they needed to protect the integrity of the IDPs. I listened to him, sipping the soft drink he had offered me from his office fridge. I understood why they had to be careful; the Nigerian army hasn't always had the greatest reputation for civility. Their notoriety for dishing out corporal punishment to civilians on the streets was firmly established during the succession of military regimes between 1966 and 1999.

Recently, there have been reports that the soldiers and vigilantes guarding the camps have been exchanging food for sex with desperate inhabitants of the camps. Some IDPs have become pregnant as a result. I found myself wondering if, desperate as she was to feed her children, Sa'adatu would eventually succumb to something similar. There is nothing hunger will not drive people to.

Without authorisation, I managed to make my way into the Bakassi Camp early the next morning.

What has become the Bakassi Camp was conceived as a luxury estate for the high and mighty. Driving in through gates manned by the military and local vigilantes, one is confronted by expansive flats stretching into the distance. They are still unpainted. Built with public funds, a government official tried to appropriate the choice real estate for private use, but after another round of elections new officials seized the property and put it to use as a camp for IDPs.

Beyond the luxury flats, endless rows of tarpaulin shelters have been set up to accommodate more and more IDPs pouring in from different parts of Borno, from areas that have been occupied or attacked by Boko Haram. Nearly thirty thousand people live in the Bakassi camp.

Sa'adatu is from Gwoza, eighty-five miles south-east of Maiduguri. In 2014, when Boko Haram was in the ascendancy, the town came under sporadic attack. Sa'adatu's husband, Musa Adamu – who had two other wives and a total of nineteen children – was just recovering from surgery and contemplating moving his family to a more secure location.

'We heard stories of "the boys" ambushing people on the way and killing them,' she said, referring to Boko Haram. Boko Haram do not like being called Boko Haram, which they see as derogatory, and those who have lived within reach of their reign of terror have found other euphemisms for them. Afraid they would be waylaid if they left, she and her family stayed on in Gwoza, hoping to ride out the trouble. But after the Eid feast of July 2014, Boko Haram tightened its grip around their town and they realised they couldn't stay any longer. The possibility of fleeing into an ambush became more enticing than waiting to be gunned down in their homes.

'If the boys had stopped us on the way, it would have been Allah's will,' she said, stirring the steaming gruel. I wondered if the meal wasn't being overcooked, when I noticed how mildly the flame was burning, licking the bottom of the pot without commitment. One of Sa'adatu's daughters, aged about ten, walked in, her skin dripping with water. She had just had her bath in one of the toilets in camp, of which there were several. Made of roofing sheets, these are strategically located to avoid overcrowding. Hand-pumped boreholes provide water, so

Sa'adatu's water-storage utensils were left empty in the corner of the room. The girl sat opposite her mother, looking into the pot while pretending to twiddle her toes.

Back in 2014, Sa'adatu had packed carefully. They took utensils, bedding and a supply of food, both cooked and uncooked. She loaded this onto the heads of her children, strapped her last born, only a few weeks old then, on her back, and together with her husband set out on foot. They trekked for two days and a night, avoiding major roads and towns, until they arrived at a military facility.

The soldiers don't know who the enemy is, because Boko Haram is not a conventional army. As a result, the family was detained and questioned for days. If they were judged to be Boko Haram sympathisers, their fate would be sealed. The saving grace, Sa'adatu said, was that someone the military trusted vouched for them.

'The man knew my husband and told them he was certain that we weren't involved with Boko Haram. He told them he knew us very well and had last seen my husband a month before,' she said.

Perhaps if he hadn't added the last sentence, things might have turned out differently. The soldiers wanted to look into that one-month window. The whole family was transferred to Giwa barracks in Maiduguri, which had become notorious as a detention centre for suspected members of the Boko Haram terror group. Amnesty International's report in May 2016 suggested that between January and May 2016, 149 people, including children as young as five months, died at Giwa.

Sa'adatu and her husband were unaware of these figures, and even if they had heard rumours about Giwa barracks' notoriety, anywhere was better than being held in Boko Haram's enclave.

Sa'adatu and her children were put in a detention cell alongside other women and minors. She estimates their numbers to have been around two hundred and eighty. There was no toilet, and since they were locked in between 4 p.m. and 9 a.m., they urinated and defecated in a huge plastic drum, which they took turns emptying in the morning.

The men were held in a separate building. They were not let out. So in the hours that the cell doors were thrown open to her, Sa'adatu went round the back of the men's detention building to catch glimpses of her husband through the window.

'I would wave at him and he would wave back,' she said, looking at the UNHCR logo printed on the white tarpaulin wall as if she could see his face there. 'When his shirt was dirty, he would take it off and throw it through the window. I would wash it and throw it back to him so the soldiers didn't see.'

After two months at Giwa, her husband sent her a message. He had heard they were going to be transferred to another facility for further interrogation. 'He asked me and the children to fast and pray for him,' she said. Sa'adatu was also worried. She had heard stories by now from other detainees, and from the soldiers too.

'We were told that during the previous government, the men were taken and shot. But now things are better so they are only taken to be questioned. Those who are not involved in the insurgency might get out in five months. So don't worry, they said, if your husband is innocent, he will be out in months. But we were told that if death comes, whether you are in your home or in the market, it will meet you. Some of the men may die before those five months are up.'

The next morning, Sa'adatu and the other women watched as a vehicle escorted by armed soldiers took the men away. With her little boy balanced on her hip, she watched the convoy drive towards the gates and recede into the distance, wondering when she would see her husband again. She was sure she would see him again. He had nothing the soldiers wanted; he was innocent. She was certain of that. But ten long months have passed since that day. Her little baby has grown into a toddler, and Sa'adatu's husband has not returned.

'We took ourselves there,' she said, her voice trailing off. 'By ourselves, we took ourselves there.'

Two months after her husband was shipped out of Giwa barracks, Sa'adatu and her children were crammed into a vehicle and moved to the Arabic Teachers' College camp, where over a year later hunger would drive the IDPs into the streets. She only stayed twenty days. The truck came for her again and this time she was moved to the Bakassi Camp, where another ten thousand people from Gwoza were kept. Sa'adatu felt better back among familiar faces, comforted by people who knew for certain her husband was only a victim, just as they all were.

But here, at Bakassi, new challenges arose. In the eight months she has been at the camp, the stores have remained empty. The last time supplies were replenished was over a year ago, months before she arrived. Relief materials are scarce, and the IDPs are not allowed to go out and beg for food or alms. Maiduguri is laden with whispers – whispers of trucks loaded with relief materials driving in through the front gates of the camps, and then driving out the rear gates, still fully loaded.

Sometimes, Sa'adatu strolls by the camp kitchen to see if the hearth is being stoked in preparation for a meal. But the ashes have been cold for weeks now and she often returns with tears stinging in her eyes, unsure what to tell the children. And with the exits from the camps tightly controlled by the soldiers and vigilantes, her chances of going out to beg for food on the streets are curtailed, and the possibility of getting news of her husband increasingly remote.

Rumours of a possible relocation to Gwoza, which might happen by the end of the year, do not excite her as they do the other IDPs, who think that back home they might be able to find food more regularly. The way Sa'adatu sighed at the rumours, I suspected a return home might have appealed if her husband was with her.

'I don't know where my husband is, whether he is dead or alive,' she said, her head cocked to one side in a posture of resignation. The room is silent now, completely, save for the wheezing breath of her hungry children sleeping on the empty sacks on the floor.

The drive across Maiduguri was laced with silence, that kind of brooding, contemplative silence in which one takes stock of things, such as the essence of life and hunger and death. Classic country music rolled out of the car speakers, filling the void. Every time the car slowed down in traffic, hordes of children, and sometimes adults too, clawed at the windows, begging for charity.

'Please help an orphan,' they each chanted, shuffling against each other, trying to position themselves better for whatever might come out of the car. There are many of them now in Maiduguri. So many it bothers you. They are the orphans of the Boko Haram carnage, and those who pose as such victims to make some money. There will always be people who take advantage.

Beyond the forest of outstretched arms and clawing fingers, Maiduguri seemed normal, almost – a city learning to breathe again after the ravages of Boko Haram. Traders and artisans have goods on display in shops and walkways. Fancy street lamps line the roads, some imported from France to give the city the exotic ambience of Paris. I am surprised by how boisterous the city seems, bulging with life and hordes of displaced people. And the dreams that people have, even in the most troubling times.

It was here that what has become known today as Boko Haram was born, here in this city of the proud Kanuri tribe and their ancient history, the seat of the Kanem Empire. It was here that one Muhammed Yusuf started preaching a radical form of Islam in 2002, exponentially growing his militant fan base with frustrated youths. And when in 2009 the group confronted the authorities, it was here, in Maiduguri, that they were brutally crushed. Yusuf was killed along with hundreds of his followers. Other members of his sect fled and went underground, only to resurface in 2011 as the deadly terror group that would, at the peak of its powers (around January 2015), hold some twenty thousand square miles of territory – an area roughly the size of Croatia.

Our car is stopped now at a checkpoint. Young vigilantes armed with bamboo clubs, machetes and Dane guns peer into the car, looking at me, my photographer and the driver. Their bleary eyes and dope-stained lips tell of drug use. They are called the Civilian Joint Task Force. Tired of Boko Haram attacks, youths of the city took up arms to hunt down the terrorists that had risen from among them. And it is in large part thanks to them that Maiduguri is relatively free of the insurgents. The model has been replicated in other towns in the north-east, helping the military to identify and tackle members of the sect. The story of this insurgency cannot be told without their contribution, but when Boko Haram is fully subjugated, the government will have to find some use for these youths, or they too will become a problem.

For now, they are everywhere, patrolling the streets and guarding buildings. They were there at the gate of the Dalori IDP camp on the outskirts of the city, where they and the soldiers keep watch.

Dalori is one of the biggest camps in the country. Walking through the gate, one is confronted by hordes of people and endless rows of tarpaulin shelters that stretch as far as the eyes can see.

Zahra Mohammed, a twenty-five-year-old Cameroonian, lives here. Her shack is just a single room, about six feet by ten feet. Her personal effects – plates, mats and a flimsy mattress – are scattered around the little space. You can hear voices through the tarpaulin walls separating her from her neighbours.

In the year Zahra has lived here, her life has consisted of waking up, washing her dishes, cleaning her room and, at about noon, joining the queues for the first meal of the day.

'Sometimes we don't get food, so we try to cook whatever we have scavenged or some of the relief materials we have,' she says. She is soft-spoken, but there is sharpness in her eyes, eyes that belie the difficult times she has gone through, both here and in the forest she was rescued from.

Herwa Community Development Initiative, the NGO that offers her counselling and trains her and others in skill acquisition, euphemistically calls her a survivor. Others who are less tactful would call her a 'Boko Haram Wife'.

In July 2014, Zahra was recently divorced, nursing her seven-month-old baby Jamila and tending to her sick mother at a hospital in Kolofata, northern Cameroon, when she heard gunshots and explosions.

Armed men burst in, pointed their guns at her, then dragged Zahra and her child away from her mother's bedside. She was blindfolded and thrown into a truck along with other women. One of them was the wife of the Cameroonian deputy prime minister Amadou Ali, and it was primarily because of her that the Boko Haram attack on Kolofata made the local and international news. Not one of these reports mentioned Zahra Mohammed by name. She was one of the 'other women'.

Zahra's heart beat wildly as they drove, and she heard the sounds of the life she used to know recede into the distance. They bumped their way through rough bush paths, on and on until all that was familiar was only a memory, save her daughter clinging to her.

They were driven into the forest of Buni Yadi, where the younger women were separated from the older ones. That was the last time Zahra would see the wife of the deputy prime minister, even though they were held together for three months. Every day, armed men would escort the younger women to attend classes run by Boko Haram scholars. And when new victims were captured in raids, the militants asked Zahra and the other captives to cook for them. There was a routine to that life in Buni Yadi, but that routine was soon disrupted.

One day, bombs fell out of the heavens and exploded around the militants' camp. Screaming, the terrified women crouched on the floors, fearing a bomb would explode over their heads and that would be the end of it. But they survived.

The air raid forced Boko Haram to move camp, relocating with their hostages to another forest. At the new camp, Zahra worried about the well-being of her daughter, her son, who had been with his father when she was taken, and the fate of her ill mother left in the hospital. Her captors were contemplating other matters.

'They said they wanted to marry me,' Zahra said. 'I told them I wanted to return to my parents, and they said my parents were infidels and I would never see them again.' It was a curious proposal. If Zahra had said yes, the interested militant would have reported to the amir, or the head of the cell, that he had found a willing wife. For Boko Haram, hierarchy is important. A witness – a survivor – had told me she had seen about twenty militants executed by their commander for taking 'wives' without his consent. They were branded fornicators and shot. Against the wishes of the executioner, the women were spared because they were forced into the 'marriage'. The enraged executioner had to be physically restrained from shooting the women.

Zahra did not know this, of course, but she still rejected the proposal. Spurned, the militants decided to force her hand.

'They put me in a hole in the ground and covered it with some crude construct. They kept me there for fifteen days. And when they brought me out, I still refused,' she said. She was fiddling with her fingers now.

She sat staring out of the door to where the other women were sitting in the shade, braiding their hair and speaking in Kanuri. I imagined how she must have felt in those seven months of her captivity, losing all contact with home and everyone she had loved. I wondered if she heard when the government of Cameroon negotiated with Boko Haram for the release of the wife of the deputy prime minister. If she had wished she was with those freed alongside the wife of the politician after the ransom was paid. I wondered how it felt to be one of the forgotten ones, and to remain one of the forgotten ones years later.

With no news of home, all she had was her daughter, Jamila. She held her for comfort at night and the innocent child, then fourteen months old, was the only source of joy she had.

But then the fighter jets came again. Another day, another raid. With bombs dropping, chaos broke out in the camp. The women saw an opening and fled into the forest, but were pursued by their unrelenting captors.

With little Jamila strapped to her back, Zahra ran into uncharted terrain. The wrapper she used to bind her daughter to her back came undone and Jamila tumbled off, falling to the ground and snapping her neck.

I could visualise Zahra falling to her knees, shaking her baby, asking her to wake up, calling her name and wailing to the heavens. But Jamila was dead. And when the Boko Haram militants caught up with the distraught woman, they dragged her away.

'Your crying will not bring her back,' they told her.

There was something almost mechanical about the way Zahra narrated her story, as if wanting to detach herself from it. Perhaps it was because she had already told it several times before, to her fellow refugees and displaced persons, to newshounds, NGOs and the international aid groups who had promised to help her find her family, all without success.

The only moment emotion crept into her voice was when she said, 'I still think about my daughter.' She looked down at her fingers, now dovetailed into each other. 'I think about her all the time.'

When another military raid on their new camp at Kera Laji presented another opportunity to escape, Zahra took it. Survival was paramount in her mind. She ran. For her dead daughter. For her living son. For her sick mother, who may or may not be dead. For the love of life, she ran and did not stop, until she, along with five other women, reached Bama, which had just been retaken by the Nigerian Army.

There they were housed in the local prison for five days, until Boko Haram made a spirited attempt to retake the city. The attack was repelled and the army decided it was best to move the women to the safety of Maiduguri, to the massive camp of Dalori, where Zahra has been ever since.

It was Tuesday. In the bright sun of Maiduguri, close to the gate of the Dalori camp, there was a football match going on, two teams of IDPs slugging it out against each other. But for Zahra, it was just another day.

She had woken up to the humdrum life of the camp. And by noon, it was clear there wouldn't be any food that day. The cooks were idling in the kitchen, cleaning utensils and finding ways of appearing busy, but anyone could tell nothing was happening. Zahra would have to cook some of her rice or noodles. She had some spice she could sprinkle on them to give them a little taste. Conditions at Dalori are far better than at the Bakassi camp; at least here, food is more regular and the prospect of starving does not loom so large.

When she was told that some officials from Herwa, the NGO that has been counselling her, had come and were waiting for her at the United Nations Population Fund (UNFPA) tent, she probably didn't think much of it. She shelved her plans to cook for the moment. Who knew, perhaps the kitchen would come alive by the time she was done.

The UNFPA tent was located near the makeshift school in the camp. It stood out from the field of white tarpaulins because it was yellow and the sunlight streaming through the tarp gave the inside of the tent an ethereal amber glow.

There was only one Herwa official on the ground, but he had come with representatives of the Federation of Muslim Women's Associations in Nigeria (FOMWAN).

The women huddled on the mats in the middle of the tent, talking to the officials. Soon, there was a buzz of excitement. Other women who had been in separate corners joined the group in the centre. Zahra sat, her hands on her lap, looking down at the mat. She seemed dazed.

One of the FOMWAN officials was also Cameroonian, and she happened to know Zahra's parents. She told Zahra that her mother had recovered from her illness; her family had relocated to Marwa, but they were alive and well.

It was the first news from home Zahra had received in two years. Looking at her sitting there in the midst of the women, holding back the tears in her eyes, I could see how much this bit of news meant to her. She seemed completely floored by this happy coincidence.

'They think I am dead,' Zahra told me later. 'They told them I had been killed in one of the air raids in the forest. They've even said prayers for my soul.'

This information was hard for her to process and she didn't seem to know how to handle the news. But beneath the confusion, there was relief. And the renewed stirring of hope, the thawing of dreams long put on ice. There would be bureaucracy and paperwork to get her out of the camp if someone came for her, but the priority now was to reach out to her parents and let them know she was alive.

'I just want to see my family and my son again,' she said. The trembling in her voice told of anxiety, of an eagerness to remove the cloak of death from over her head, to reveal herself to the world she knew and that knew her.

For Zahra, there is now a glimmer of light at the end of her long and winding tunnel. For Sa'adatu Musa and her children at Bakassi, the wait continues.

THE REFUGEE

LIVING IN A VOID

KHALED KHALIFA

Translated from the Arabic by Jonathan Wright

KHALED KHALIFA was born in Aleppo, Syria, in 1964 and currently lives in Damascus. His 1993 debut novel, entitled *Haris al-khadi'a* [The Guard of Deception] was followed by *Dafatir al-Qurbat* [The Gypsies' Notebooks] in 2000, *In Praise of Hatred* in 2006 (published in English by Black Swan) and *No Knives in the Kitchens of this City* in 2013 (published in English by The American University in Cairo Press). He was shortlisted for the 2008 and 2014 International Prize for Arabic Fiction and is the winner of the Naguib Mahfouz Medal for Literature.

JONATHAN WRIGHT was a journalist with Reuters for almost thirty years, mostly in the Middle East. For the past ten years he has been translating Arabic literature, mainly contemporary fiction, including works by Youssef Ziedan, Hassan Blassim, Amjad Nasser, Saud Alsanoussi and Alaa Al Aswany. He studied Arabic at Oxford University.

MY sister, whom I haven't seen for more than two years, told me she was going to cross the sea in a rubber dinghy. Then she hung up. She didn't want to hear what I thought. She merely said something profound and sentimental and entrusted her three children to my care in the event that she drowned. A few minutes later, I tried to call the unfamiliar Turkish number back, but the phone had been turned off. Hundreds of images from our childhood flooded my memory. It's not easy to say goodbye to half a century of your life and wait for someone you love to drown. My fingers and toes felt cold and my head empty. I didn't feel able to argue anyway. What can one offer a woman who has lost her home and everything she owned and who carried her children off into exile, to seek a safe haven in Turkish towns, so as not to lose them too? Things are not easy for women like her in Turkey. She looks like millions of other Syrian women and does not have any special skills. All that's left is the hope of asylum, even if it requires crossing the sea in a rubber dinghy. It's as if she's trying to tell me something I know already – that the sea is the Syrian's only hope.

Maybe it was luck that saved my sister. She didn't drown and she found friends to help her in Greece and the other countries she passed through. She certainly didn't talk about any unpleasant experiences with traffickers who fleeced her of what little money she had or left her destitute in airport waiting rooms. In any case, she eventually reached her destination and in Denmark she hooked up with a group of friends who lent her a helping hand. Some of her fellow adventurers had drowned in scenes of unimaginable horror. Death may take many forms, but the bleakest and blackest of them all is death by drowning, which is a complete denial of everything the human body stands for. The drowned body becomes food for the fishes of the sea and dissolves like salt in a bowl of water.

In the days that followed, I received a similar message from my younger brother, who had left his home in Aleppo and gone to Mersin, where he left his family and sailed alone, embarking on an arduous journey that extended from Greece to Italy and finally to Sweden. Then came an endless stream of phone calls, from friends and close relatives, including cousins, all telling me they were about to set sail. I no longer asked for details of the journey or discussed it with them. I wished them a safe trip and asked them to put our minds at rest when they arrived safely. Hundreds of thousands of Syrians are still thinking along the same lines. In coffee shops in Turkish towns and cities, they exchange telephone numbers of traffickers and information about the best routes. They post this kind of information on Facebook, sometimes even in open forums.

I remember travelling from Damascus to Istanbul through Beirut airport in the summer of 2015, and how I was struck by the profile of the passengers, who almost all conformed to the same types. There was a large group of young people no more than twenty years old and a group of women with only their children. To me they looked like childhood friends or relatives. It was clear from their questions that they were travelling abroad for the first time. After the plane left Damascus airport, they breathed a sigh of relief and started talking aloud about their plans for the future. They were travelling to Istanbul and then boarding another plane to the city closest to the Greek border. Most of these young people were avoiding military service and enjoying the luxury of flying by air for the first time. Their journey seemed to be prearranged. I noticed there was a man in his forties who gave them instructions after the plane took off from Damascus bound for Beirut, and in the transit lounge at Beirut airport the same thing happened. The women were receiving the same instructions. I thought of those youngsters, whose only hope now was to set sail across the sea. It wasn't strange to me, but it was interesting, despite the anguish, that a group of friends should choose to emigrate as a group. I remembered our dreams when we were young and how we promised each other as a group of friends to be eternally faithful and how we planned our lives communally. These young people had decided to live or die together. Their eyes betrayed their fear, but together they managed to be braver. I watched them summon mutual support as they got ready to face the monster.

Most of my friends have left the country and are now refugees. All I can do is look for the names of the missing and the drowned and track my friends' new addresses. Whenever a boat sinks I find myself spinning like a madman, desperately searching for information, for lists of the drowned and any details about them – which towns or villages they were from, their family names, pictures of them. Again in 2015, I went through the same hysterical search for the faces of detained friends among the photographs of the dead leaked from the regime's prisons, known as the 'Caesar' photographs, after the codename of the photographer. I examined the absent faces on the off-chance I might find among them any of the dozens of missing friends about whom we know nothing: no news, no messages passed on by word of mouth; no one has seen them or has any information about them. I examined the pictures and when I thought I recognised someone I tried to remember other details about the person – a mole on the cheek or a scar on the knee. But it was pointless. Looking for drowned or dead people and waiting for detainees to return is an act of absurdity, one matched only by the act of living in towns awaiting their turn to be destroyed.

The throngs of people leaving continued, so much so that in 2013 and 2014 we held communal farewell parties for friends departing for the unknown. We no longer debated the options or offered them our experience of cities we knew. Leaving the country became an epidemic that swept our lives. Places began to empty of their usual customers. Everything was changing very rapidly. The streets of the city were deserted, the windows were dark and telephones went unanswered. Everything suggested imminent disaster. Everyone sensed it. I started to suffer from an overwhelming sense of loss, I felt I was losing all my friends and there was nothing I could do about it. Just like everyone else left inside the country, I was busy staying alive. We no longer thought about who would leave. The question had changed to: 'When are you going to leave?' Or: 'Why are you still here?' For the first time we had a taste of mass dispersion.

At first I didn't believe they wouldn't all come back. I thought their departure would be temporary. But after all these years I've arranged my life around their absence. The gap they left has been filled by another gap. I no longer think about how they look now. People like me, who live with characters they invent on paper and who celebrate imagination, cannot feel impotent. So I've become more attached to my life here and started to worry about being infected by the plague of displacement that has proliferated with the despair I see in people's faces every morning. I ask myself whether I would stay here if my house was destroyed. I don't have an answer, but recently I've begun to come to terms with the idea. Yes, I would remain, but why? I don't know the answer, or I'm embarrassed by the knowledge that I simply want to cling to a place that has a smell I know well. Ultimately, these are the delusions of a solitary writer, one who no longer has anything to lose having observed, at length, Syrians attempt to win back their country, then lose everything. It's as if the price Syrians must pay to recover their freedom and dignity includes every last stone, tree, nook and cranny, so that Syrians cannot, in fact, win back their country from the clutches of the dictatorship. They have lived in the shadow of that dictatorship for fifty years, during which time they've invented endless ways to resist it and coexist with its decay, at the very least by holding their tongues and waiting, defending a civic culture that is thousands of years old.

In recent years I have received many invitations, travelled across the world and met Syrians who emigrated years ago. I have observed their lives and concluded that refugees lose their identity but do not acquire a new one. Abandoning a small set of habits that constitute personal contentment would be intolerable to me. I'm thinking of my morning coffee at home or coffee with my friends before going to work, chatting, of the city's smells, dinners, the smell of rain in autumn. My refugee friends celebrated all these things, but then they abandoned them. And in recent months our phone calls and our messages via Facebook and email have become less frequent. The fall of the first rain in Damascus is no longer the occasion for a festival of nostalgia in which hundreds of thousands of refugees across the world take part. Our moments together are now few and far between, and we haven't spoken much about the problems of assimilating into an alien culture, about the idea of abandoning one's original identity. I understand their frustrations and the extent of the difficulties they face, and at the same time I understand their concern for us – we who have chosen to stay where war lies in wait for us on every corner.

I have not abandoned my emotions, and I don't want to speak from a sociological perspective, because if you research the subject of Syrian refugees you find there is something that distinguishes them from other refugees, which is to do with their multiplicity of cultures and classes, but would take hundreds of pages to explain. I would like to say something along the lines of how the refugees are Syria's loss and the world's gain, but I'm not sure that's entirely true. Abandoning one's identity is like ripping a heart out of a body. I think of the families of friends who have migrated en masse. For example, I received a phone call from the father of a refugee friend, a man over seventy years old, who spoke to me in tears. He just wanted to speak to someone who understood his language, who understood the secrets of the language, who would listen to a joke in his version of colloquial Syrian and who would have a hearty laugh with him. A hearty laugh – that's a metaphor for the way people like to live, and refugees in general are not that lucky, especially in their first years in exile. But then the phones stopped ringing. Everyone had dropped into the black hole of exile. At first there were hundreds of them, then thousands, then hundreds of thousands, and now millions of refugees. I'm horrified by the pictures coming out of countries that don't welcome the refugees, by pictures of fascists threatening refugees, by posters put up in some Lebanese towns imposing a curfew on Syrians after six o'clock in the evening, by posters that openly insult refugees. I'm horrified by that Hungarian journalist who kicked a Syrian man carrying a child, running away from a war he did not choose. The same journalist was nevertheless recently awarded a prize. I'm horrified by these pictures and by a prize being awarded to someone who kicks my countrymen. I think of those people with whom I claim to be acquainted. I think of their suffering, but at the same time I'm overwhelmed and I can't understand what's happening. I don't want to surrender to the idea that we will wake up one day to find the city deserted – no people, no houses with lights on, no cars. And if we ask what happened we'll simply discover that everyone contributed to us becoming a society of refugees.

The picture seems murky and incomprehensible to people who haven't met Syrians before or who don't know anything about the modern or ancient history of Syria. Over the past hundred years, Syria has taken in large numbers of refugees, displaced people and people fleeing death. At the beginning of the last century, the Syrians took in Armenians, Chechens and Albanians who were fleeing massacres and wars, and they later received more than half a million Palestinians after the disaster of 1948 and the war of June 1967. The process reached its climax when Syria accepted more than three million displaced Iraqis in 2003 after Baghdad was occupied by the Americans. In the war of 2006, Syrians took in hundreds of thousands of Lebanese. Syria has not closed its borders to refugees for a single day since the beginning of the twentieth century, not to mention ancient migrations that have long made Syria a country that draws refugees. Numerous different peoples have settled in the country and made it their eternal home.

Throughout the last century, Syria was also a place from which people emigrated, but not as refugees. The big migrations in the late nineteenth and early twentieth century saw hundreds of thousands of Syrians leave for the United States and countries in Latin America. These economic migrations were, on the whole, a significant success, and the latest statistics circulating in 2006 spoke of twenty million people of Syrian origin in the diaspora, most of them in Argentina and Brazil. The circumstances that forced these migrants to leave their country were completely different from those faced by today's refugees, who will end up numbering more than seven million people. Most of them live in camps in Jordan and Lebanon in conditions of unimaginable misery and deprivation. Even if the refugees in the Turkish camps seem to be better off, the magnitude of the problems they face cannot be ignored, especially when it comes to children's schooling, for a whole generation of Syrians will be deprived of education. The situation is better for the lucky ones whose boats have not sunk and who have managed to reach countries in Europe that are sympathetic towards refugees, such as Germany and France. But in general, it's impossible to imagine how bad conditions are for the great mass of refugees, such as those who live in the Zaatari camp in Jordan, and how deprived they are of their most basic human rights. On top of that there is the constant threat that the borders will be closed in the face of people fleeing the continuing war.

But one must also remember that for the past fifty years Syria has been a country that expels its own citizens. For the past fifty years violent repression by the regime and its denial of the most basic human rights have turned Syria, under President Hafez al-Assad and his son, into a kingdom of fear and dread, causing a constant outflow of talented Syrians. Hundreds of thousands of Syrians live in the Gulf States and millions of Syrians are acquiring their higher education in Europe and America, and will live out their lives there. These statistics are horrifying for a small country such as Syria, which measures 185,000 square kilometres and had 24 million inhabitants in 2011. Some people say there are 10,000 Syrian doctors in France alone, and they talk about the same number in the United States and other countries. The regime has not only driven these talented people into exile: it has even pursued them in their places of refuge and prevented them from assembling. It has planted suspicion among them, threatened them through family members still living in Syria, deprived them of the chance to visit their mother country, and thwarted persistent efforts by exiled Syrians to find out about one another and form pressure groups in the countries they now live in. Emigrant and exiled Syrians have always seemed to be in a sorry state compared to other groups who have been through the same experience but been able to hold together, support each other and help propagate their original culture. The experience of Argentines who fled their country in the 1970s, for example, might be compared to that of Syrians to understand just how difficult the latter's exile has been.

What Syrians still cannot understand is how they have been transformed from a people that received refugees into refugees themselves, people who suffer bitterly wherever they go. Borders are closed in their faces. Their clothing, their hearts and the lines on their hands are examined in detail. Anyone who has witnessed this horrific ritual will also have seen how the world, after abandoning the Syrians and even allowing them to be slaughtered, murdered and drowned, suddenly finds cause for sympathy in a single photograph – such as the picture of young Alan dead on the beach. The picture shook the world for several days, but was then filed away, just as attempts to find reasons for the Syrian tragedy and ways to bring it to an end have been. A similar picture will show up from time to time, and through it the world will be able to offer its sympathy for people living under bomb raids by Russian and Syrian air force planes. This has been going on for five years, without the world thinking seriously about how to stop the constant bloodshed. Syria is the victim of a public execution, and turning a whole people into refugees would seem to be the hidden reason for not stopping this war, or rather for supporting its continuation by creating ready-made enemies that convince large segments of the public in Europe, America and other parts of the world that it is too difficult to solve the issue. The formation of Islamic State/Daesh is but one piece of horrible evidence that the world has abandoned its moral duty to support people in their struggle for peace and democracy.

Although asking questions is a central principle of European culture and modernity, questioning, in this case, appears to be forbidden. No one is asking who created a fascistic, dreadful and criminal organisation such as Daesh, who has financed it, who enabled it to occupy whole cities and who turned a blind eye to swarms of Daesh fighters crossing the desert between the Syrian city of Raqqa and the Iraqi city of Mosul. This organisation's vehicles move in a disciplined manner and in long convoys, behaving like a proper state with a sovereignty that the world respects. The fact that these questions are not seriously posed today will destroy all the values of civilisation that humanity has defended and paid a heavy price to establish. I mean values of justice, accountability for war crimes, democracy and the right to self-determination. This is what has happened. Mankind has abandoned its values. There is now a terrifying ghoul called Daesh, which people are always talking about destroying and saying how hard it will be. It is one of the reasons why millions of refugees have gone into exile and whole cities have been depopulated. In the very near future the idea of installing new ethnicities, nationalities and sects in place of other sects and ethnicities might become acceptable, or the price to pay for stopping the war and the bloodshed of innocent civilians, while no one speaks about the role of the regime and its allies.

The issue in Syria is not one of refugees but of a whole population either being turned into corpses or forced to flee while the world stands silently by. And of the lies circulated by heads of state, especially Western ones, about the need to protect civilians and not force inhabitants out of their towns and villages, familiar statements issued to ease the conscience of those who make and promote them, but ineffective in stopping war and bringing criminals to international justice.

Images don't disappear easily, and it brings me little satisfaction to meet friends I have lost touch with when I visit the cities they now live in. I remember when I was in Oslo, in 2013, and a refugee friend of mine came to where I was taking part in a seminar. It was too much for her and she cried throughout the seminar, and seeing her in tears was too much for me. The seminar came to a halt for a few minutes, but it was difficult to explain the emotions that we shared, the bitterness of exile, the uprooting of a person from their rightful place. Many people have not chosen their new lives, but have been forced to live them. The majority will live on social benefits provided by their countries of exile and many will live in order to bring up a new generation, one that is robust and acclimatised to their new life, a generation, however, that will not know the meaning of the life their fathers and mothers once lived. Two lives, side by side, that will not merge, however hard they try. And the story will not end until all the eyewitnesses have died, until fathers and grandfathers are dead, so that children living in refuge can be at peace in their new environment, enjoying their attachment to their acquired identity. But until these witnesses die we have to imagine a chord of hope that will stretch from Berlin and other German, French, Turkish and Scandinavian cities, to towns and villages throughout Syria.

My brother has now obtained the right to reunite his family and he cannot hide his happiness that the pain of separation will now come to an end. He is learning Swedish, which I doubt he will master for he is almost fifty years old, and my sister is learning Danish, and in the best-case scenario she will learn a few dozen phrases that will enable her to buy bunches of parsley for the tabbouleh she makes so well, and to explain how to make it to her neighbours, who won't visit her and won't ask after her if she dies alone. Her death might not even cause a stir, whereas in our culture the whole family would be shamed if they allowed one of its members to die alone.

The rest of my friends are trying, by various means, to assure us that they are happy in their new places of exile. Meanwhile, those of us who have stayed are dropping one by one, family by family, so much so that the idea of an empty city could become a reality within a few years. But I remain convinced that refugees lose their sense of identity, for they cannot obtain a new one or completely forget their old one. To be a refugee is to live in a void – it is to lead a painful life, however hard we try to embellish it.

BELIZE

THE SALVADORAN PROMISED LAND

JUAN JOSÉ MARTÍNEZ D'AUBUISSON

Translated from the Spanish by Frances Riddle

The anthropologist and author JUAN JOSÉ MARTINEZ D'AUBUISSON was born in El Salvador in 1986 and has researched the phenomena of gang crime and its effects on his country for over ten years. He has written literary reports for multiple media formats. He published his first book of stories in 2010, *Las mujeres que nadie amó* [The Women No One Loved], which was followed in 2015 by his non-fiction work entitled *Ver, oír y callar* [See, Hear and Be Silent].

FRANCES RIDDLE lives in Buenos Aires, Argentina, where she works as a translator, writer and editor. She holds an MA in Translation Studies from the University of Buenos Aires and a BA in Spanish Literature. Her book-length publications include *A Simple Story* by Leila Guerriero (New Directions, 2017); *Bodies of Summer* by Martín Felipe Castagnet (Dalkey Archive Press, 2017); *Slum Virgin* by Gabriela Cabezón Cámara (Charco Press, 2017); and *The Life and Deaths of Ethel Jurado* by Gregorio Casamayor (Hispabooks, 2017).

FOR the northern triangle of Central America, Belize is like the little pig that built his house out of bricks: whenever the wolf of violence appears, Central Americans run to their neighbour for safety. It seems especially true of the Salvadorans, who have been less exacting in their construction methods. During El Salvador's political-military conflict in the 1980s, thousands of refugees fled to Belize. There they were taken in, given land, and called Belizeans. Now a new wave of violence torments the smallest country in the region and once again the compass points north, to the warm, tropical land that has so often provided safe haven.

In August 2014, Alma's brother was shot several times by Salvadoran gang members as he drove his moto-taxi. The bullets didn't take his life immediately; he lay there 'gasping', his family members say, like a fish out of water. The ambulance took too long to arrive and the twenty-three-year-old man died from blood loss before he reached the hospital. His family then fled El Salvador for fear that they too would be left gasping for air.

In June 2016, Jaime likewise felt forced to leave the country. Gang members in his neighbourhood of San Salvador began demanding a weekly payment that was too much for him to afford with his small business of home-made hamburgers and hot dogs. A group of boys he'd known since they were children showed up at his house one night to kill him. He was miraculously able to save his own life. The next day he sold everything and left El Salvador along with his six-year-old daughter, aiming to get as far away as possible from the pack of children that had taken his business away from him.

Wendy, nine years old, also had a problem, a big one, with the Mara Salvatrucha 13, undoubtedly the largest gang in the Americas, probably in the world. Her family turned to the police for help and were advised to leave the country if they wanted to live. Wendy narrowly escaped, along with her parents and her grandmother, and managed to survive.

The same thing happened to Marlon and Jessica and Carlos and Bryan, and the young farmer from western El Salvador who left to avoid ending up, like many of his friends, under the ground he tilled or in one of the clandestine cemeteries of the Barrio 18 gang.

They all went to Belize. Without really knowing where the chunk of land those six letters represented even was.

Wedged between dense vegetation and the Mennonites' vast fields of corn, an hour's drive down dirt roads from Belmopan, lies the Valley of Peace. It's a speck of a town in the middle of the jungle, inhabited almost entirely by Salvadorans. These families escaped from El Salvador in the 1980s. In the midst of the civil war, there was no telling which direction the bullets would come from or which side those pulling you from your house in the middle of the night would be on. Many towns and cities were razed by bombings, others became ghost towns after the inhabitants fled en masse to a less dangerous place. The military recruited boys aged twelve or younger, as soon as they could hold a rifle. The guerrillas did the same and there seemed to be no place in El Salvador for those who weren't on one of the two sides. The only option for such people, those who wanted peace, was to flee. To take whatever would fit in their backpacks and leave the country.

Unlike other refugee camps such as Mesa Grande in Honduras, or the Nicaraguan camps, this camp isn't linked to the guerrillas; the refugees did not come from the same place and they aren't organised around any ideology. They were simply families trying to escape the death that was sweeping through every corner of their country.

Don Cirilo walks out of the house and crosses the large yard, shouts a warm hello as he approaches the front gate. He offers me a calloused and arthritic hand and he chuckles when I tell him I'm Salvadoran.

'Well, this is my town, and if you're Salvadoran it's yours too.'

His hands, after so many years gripping a machete, have lost their fingerprints, a clear sign of a life of physical labour. A life spent gripping a machine gun doesn't leave the same marks. His family was one of the first three to settle in this place.

The UNHCR, along with the government of Belize, ceded a vast stretch of territory to the displaced Salvadorans. It was nothing but dense jungle at the time, but the land was flat and the soil was fertile. A testament to this fact were the hundred-year-old trees and the impenetrable green of the vegetation. If all those plants grow here, wild and forgotten, a well-tended field of maize couldn't help but flourish… And following those first three families, three more arrived, and then twenty, and then fifty, and then…

Currently, Belize has more El Salvadoran refugees than any other country in the world. Salvadorans make up 16 per cent of the total population, and that's just those who have entered the country legally. Thousands are undocumented and there is no record of them. The other eighty-plus per cent of the Belizean population is a diverse and complex ethnic mixture. The majority are Creoles, which is to say they are descendants of African slaves and British colonists. But there is also a 2 per cent population of Chinese and about as many Garifuna, Maya and other indigenous groups, and the descendants of a migration of Germans, the Mennonites, the country's elite agro-exporters. Belize seems to have been built with the ethnic leftovers of many places.

In the Valley of Peace the streets are made of dirt, a white clay that doesn't kick up dust, and the houses are built in the rural Salvadoran style: made from adobe with a method that basically consists of moulding damp earth until it can be persuaded to become a brick, the bricks to become a house. Homes have huge gardens filled with animals and hammocks at the back. Some have preserved the traditional layout of Salvadoran farmhouses, which consist of a single room with no walls and a bathroom outside. The old shabby bus, the only bus that reaches the town, driven of course by its Salvadoran owner, drops people off and picks people up, honking its horn as if it were shouting insults across the street. It honks several times outside the house of someone who needs picking up. A woman tells the driver, 'Take me to Don Chico's, please. I have to deliver a package,' and the bus diverges from its route to pass Don Chico's house. It advances slowly as the passengers converse in a lively and effusive manner, it's like a scene from inside a school bus. Everyone seems to know each other and they make jokes, almost singing the words, substituting their fs for js like in any eastern Salvadoran village.

Don Joaquín shows up at Don Cirilo's house. He's a very small man of about eighty who arrives by bicycle wearing a hat and work boots. As soon as he sits down, he starts telling stories. His octogenarian friend enlivens them with sound effects and applause. I suspect that someone told him of my arrival and he came as fast as he could, enthused by the possibility of talking about the past. This is a favourite activity for Salvadorans, a society that up until recently was mostly illiterate and had to pass on knowledge by word of mouth.

'Look, when we got here, this was forest. It was jungle, but with hard work, we went about making something out of it. The blacks bothered us at first but never too much. Maybe on the bus they'd say something to us, but they were a little afraid of us too. Because if there's anything good about being Salvadoran, it's that we were born with our balls in the right place.'

There's not much more to tell. Life in the Valley of Peace occurs between maize harvests and mass or evangelical services, between the rains and the calm rhythmic lowing of the cows. The two elderly men say that where the plaza with the wooden playground equipment for kids is, there used to be a bar… but now it's somewhere else. They say that the young people there are hard workers. They don't get into trouble or do foolish things. They work and that's it, and if they work hard enough they can build a home to raise kids who will in turn become good farmers. I ask them about the homicides and they point in the direction of Belmopan, where a recent incident has shaken the Belizean community. The homicide, under strange circumstances, of Pastor Lucas, a well-known evangelical pastor. No, I'm asking about murders in Peace Valley. And they go silent for the first time. Don Cirilo chomps his toothless jaws as he looks at me, very surprised. Don Joaquín tells me that they don't have that problem there, in a paternal tone, as if I'd said something ridiculous. I ask them then about violence in the town and they tell me that sometimes the 'kids', when they're really drunk, will get into brawls, but they never brandish their machetes. I ask them about sexual assault crimes and they tell me that the boys and girls respect each other and keep each other company when they want to. As if someone had pushed a button, a knockout blonde walks by wearing tiny shorts and a top, listening to music on her iPod. They tell me that sometimes the *gringas* who live on a nearby farm will pass through. No one harasses them. No man follows them to try to touch them or whisper something vulgar in their ears. It's as if these women are to the Salvadorans as bonobos are to chimpanzees.

I ask them about the Salvadorans who have been coming to Belize, fleeing the gangs. They don't like the topic, they try to avoid it. They've lived here in peace since the 1980s and they worry this might change as new waves of Salvadorans arrive. They talk about the new refugees like they're the carriers of a contagious virus. The virus of violence. Finally Don Cirilo tells me that few of them settle here, most of the new refugees go to Docrón, a very poor settlement on the other side of the enormous corn fields owned by the Mennonite elite. They tell me that if I want to find refugees I should go to Docrón.

An hour by bus from Belmopan, the administrative capital of Belize, the highway crosses a dirt road. The bus goes on to the city of San Ignacio Cayo. The intersection is called Blackman Eddy, named for a man who drowned many years ago in a bend of the Belize River. It's a long road, very long, especially if you don't have a car and have to walk it. It's strange to suddenly see carts driven by white men dressed like they're from nineteenth-century Alabama. It feels like you've stepped back in time. If you're travelling by foot and wish to avoid several hours under the blazing sun, you have to hitch a ride from the farmers who pass by in their carts and tractors. After a few miles, a monument rises up, welcoming visitors to Spanish Lookout. In the early twentieth century, Mennonites fleeing restrictive living conditions in Winnipeg, Canada, came to Central America, some eventually arriving at this Caribbean outpost. They asked for land and promised to work it in exchange for, among other things, their right to live in isolation from the local population. The Spanish Lookout settlement remained hermetic for many years, with nothing but rumour and legend reaching the creole locals. These days it's a European-style rural village with large beautiful wooden houses, silver silos and huge red barns. The grass is green and hammocks or swings for kids hang from trees. Further on, about an hour's walk at a quick pace, you come to the crops that sustain this paradise. Enormous fields of corn as far as the eye can see. The road continues and the houses end and all that's left is corn. Corn to the left and corn to the right. Beyond the corn is Docrón.

Docrón is a very different kind of town, with shabby wooden houses and shacks surrounded by jungle. This is where the workers live. The majority are 'Spanish', which is what Belizeans call all Spanish speakers. Skeletal dogs come out barking and biting. Puddles are home to thriving mosquito populations as the tropical vegetation energetically gives way to muddy streets. At the end of a puddle-filled path is a very humble home. Thin, barefoot and undernourished children play out front. This is where Alma lives with her family. Alma and her sister come out to greet me. At first they seem shy and afraid. They timidly set out a chair for me and fetch two more for themselves. They begin to talk. They've lived in this country for two years. One of them has had a child here, a baby boy born nine months ago. They came to escape death. They lived in the city of Zacatecoluca, in the state of La Paz, which means 'Peace', the most paradoxical of names given conditions there: of El Salvador's fourteen states, La Paz has some of the highest rates of murder, poverty and overcrowding. To put things in context, the population of La Paz alone is equal to the entire population of Belize, a country almost four hundred square miles larger than El Salvador.

In El Salvador, Alma worked as a housekeeper. She didn't earn much, she was poor, but it was her home, she had grown up there and she knew everyone and everyone knew her. Her husband worked as a vegetable vendor. He travelled through the neighbourhoods in a small truck selling vegetables that weren't his. Her younger brother, Gustavo, drove a moto-taxi: a small, junky motorcycle with a 125-horsepower motor imported from China; fifty cents a fare for a short trip. Every day, he had to cross an invisible border, the one that divided San Juan Nonualco and Zacatecoluca. In the past, this had never been a problem, but starting in 2014, as tensions between rival gangs and between the gangs and the state increased, crossing the border between the two towns became very dangerous.

Gustavo was killed by the gang members that controlled one of the two territories. They considered him a spy since he lived on the side controlled by one gang and worked in the territory of another. The police, in atypical fashion, managed to capture Gustavo's murderer and imprison him while a prosecutor gathered evidence for the trial. That's when Alma's migration was set in motion. The next week, when she was still heartbroken and burdened with grief, a man followed Alma to the bus stop as she went to work one day, and the next day, and the next... She was told that he was the brother of the incarcerated murderer and that he was following her in order to kill her so that she couldn't testify in the trial against his brother. She became a prisoner in her own home, afraid to go to work. Then gang members in every neighbourhood began to charge her husband for the right to sell vegetables on their streets. He told them that the business didn't belong to him, that he only drove the truck. But they didn't care, they wanted their money anyway. He had to visit several areas and the gang members continually increased their charge. He ended up bringing home half his usual salary. The other half was taken by the *muchachos*, the 'boys' as they're called in El Salvador, for fear of using a different word. Even here, so far away, it's the term Alma still uses. Her family was in crisis. They were broke and the man from the bus stop was sighted closer and closer to home. So they sold everything they could, at a low price, and fled. They crossed into Guatemala with five small children, bearing whatever belongings they could carry. Someone had told them that in the far corner of Central America between Guatemala and Mexico there were no gangs, that it was easier to survive. That's how they ended up in this muddy village buffered by fields of corn.

The Salvadorans, colloquially referred to by Spanish-speakers as *guanacos*, don't only live in the Valley of Peace. There are less isolated communities such as Salvapan and Las Flores in Belmopan, the capital, where Salvadorans are integrated into the life of the city like any other resident. They organise football matches and throw patriotic parties in September to celebrate Salvadoran Independence Day. They cry when the

Salvadoran national football team loses, which is almost every time they play. They listen to songs by Salvadoran singers, such as the Hermanos Flores, and they dance to the cumbia beats of Aniceto Molina. In Las Flores, probably the largest Salvadoran community in the capital, is a bar and club called La Cabaña, the place to be for *guanaco* youth. Every night from Thursday to Sunday La Cabaña serves up music, beer and karaoke. The owners are three Salvadoran brothers who came as refugees from the civil war in the 1980s and who now take over the microphone every Friday night to sing songs by Marco Antonio Solis. The place is decorated with flags from many countries, but the blue and white of the Salvadoran flag predominate. Everywhere you look something sparkles, Christmas lights or a sign for cigarettes, as if the place has been decorated by a schizophrenic designer. There's even a fish tank, lit from within, that houses what are perhaps the most tormented fish in the world. The speakers are huge and at midnight at least a hundred young people press into the space and dance euphorically to the latest hits. Many wear El Salvador football shirts as a symbol of pride, even though they were born in Belize and their parents' homeland is nothing but a place that gets mentioned in stories told by old people.

It's Sunday and throughout the neighbourhood of Las Flores the smashing hands of *pupuseras* can be heard. If in El Salvador *pupusas* – stuffed corn tortillas – are a venerated and beloved dish, here they are like communion wafers of cheese and pork rinds, held on high as something sacred. The *guanacos* who make them are devoted to the cause. They travel all the way to San Ignacio Cayo to buy the basic ingredients from a Salvadoran family that has managed to recreate the exact chemical formula for the perfect *pupusa* cheese. The place is packed and lively. Everyone talks at once and makes jokes. Only Jaime eats in silence as he eyes me suspiciously.

Jaime takes a bite of his *pupusa* and stares at me, takes another bite and stares harder, as if trying to hit me with his eyes. His daughter hugs him tightly. They've been told that I'm from El Salvador and they look at me with blatant distrust. While everyone else in the *pupuseria* is eager to tell me about their peaceful community, Jaime breathes in deeply and prepares his first question.

'So back in El Salvador, where do you live?'

It's not a question that's asked lightly in El Salvador. All neighbourhoods, but especially the poor neighbourhoods, are controlled by one of the three main gangs that operate in the country. The place you live determines the places you can and can't go. If the gang members of one neighbourhood stop you and check your ID – and gang members do check people's IDs – and discover that you live in an 'enemy' neighbourhood, even if you don't belong to any group, you're going to have a very tough time of it. You may even lose your life.

I answer and then tell him that I'm an anthropologist and that I'm writing about Salvadoran migration to Belize. Jaime relaxes a bit and tells me his story.

'I've been here barely three months. I lived in San Salvador, in Soyapango. That's where I had my business; I sold sandwiches, hot dogs and hamburgers. I'd had my business there for years and, you're not asking, but I can tell you, things weren't going too badly for me. I owned my own house. I had a car and a motorcycle. I'm separated from her mother' – he points to his daughter – 'so she and I are pretty much all there is by way of family. And, you won't believe it, but they'd never charged *la renta* on my business.'

Jaime utters this last phrase like a man who's swum with sharks without getting bitten. Soyapango is one of the most violent neighbourhoods in the Salvadoran capital, with the largest gang presence of anywhere in the country. The Mara Salvatrucha 13 (MS-13) rule the outskirts of the neighbourhood and the Barrio 18 (B-18) gang control the downtown areas and central market. Every person who conducts business in Soyapango, from the largest Coca-Cola distributor to the smallest candy stall, must pay the corresponding gang a regular tariff, popularly known as '*la renta*'.

'One day these kids came in, kids I'd watched grow up, and they told me I had to pay *la renta*. I told them to leave me the hell alone. I'd never had to pay before and why should I have to give them my money? They started to harass me. They would show up at night outside my house, and finally one day they came to kill me. They kicked the door in and I had to escape through a window. I was alone that day, if my little girl had been there... I wouldn't have got away in time. I spent the whole night in hiding and the next morning I decided to leave. I sold everything I had. My car, my motorcycle, the business. Four thousand dollars I got for all that. It's not even half what it's worth, but as I needed the money for our trip...'

In his new home in Belize, Jaime works in construction. He doesn't like it very much, it's a hard job that he's never done before. He lives in Las Flores and while he has a peaceful life, paranoia from the trauma still haunts him. A short while ago a young man found out Jaime had come over from El Salvador and said, in what may have been an ill-conceived attempt at a joke, 'Hey, man, what gang are you with?', before making the Mara Salvatrucha 13 sign with his hands. It took several neighbours to pull Jaime off the guy.

They say Jaime was shouting, 'Damn you, because of you I lost everything, everything. That business was mine, son of a bitch.' Jaime doesn't remember any of it.

The Belizean government has so far been kind to its less fortunate neighbours. They welcomed the Salvadorans who fled the civil war decades ago and they now welcome those who flee the gang wars that some experts have oversimplified with the term 'social conflict'. In cooperation with the Belizean government, the offices of the UNHCR provide refugees with temporary identification cards and process families as asylum seekers. Belmopan is a growing city; the construction sector is booming and industry in general has been developing rapidly for the past several years. This growth requires many hands willing to work, something El Salvador has in surplus. In the Belizean states of Corozal and Orange Walk there are hundreds of Salvadorans working in the vegetable and sugarcane fields. Belize also has a large number of tourist destinations along its coasts and islands, known as 'cayes'. Thousands of tourists from Europe and the US fill the beaches, nature reserves and the majestic Blue Hole, a strange *cenote,* or underwater cave. Keeping all this running smoothly requires lots of work, and that's exactly what the refugees need.

The avalanche of Salvadorans fleeing gangs is a phenomenon felt throughout the entire region. Bullets have set the population in motion and there's a mass relocation of people in this corner of the Americas. One of the main characteristics of this migration, prompted more by violence than poverty, is that those on the move are the youngest members of society, mostly children and adolescents, and they suffer the worst. The history of Salvadoran refugees fleeing to Belize seems to be repeating itself. In the 1980s, it was people who did not wish to be a part of the political conflict between Communist guerrillas and the military regime. Today it's people who do not wish to be embroiled in a gang conflict between the Mara Salvatrucha 13 and the Barrio 18. Belize seems to be a magnet for people seeking peace.

In 2014, the UNHCR met specifically to address the waves of refugees entering Belize to escape gang violence, redefining the terms under which it was possible to assign refugee status. The rules of the 1980s became obsolete in the face of the new gang wars. Every morning dozens of Salvadorans and other Central Americans arrive at the UNHCR offices and wait in line to plead their cases. Some bring documents or articles clipped from newspapers to prove their stories; others have nothing more than their word and a photo of some murdered family member.

Entire families squeeze together in the shade of the building's roof to protect themselves from the sun as they wait their turn. Today, one of those families is Wendy's.

It all began at a state school in Santa Ana, in hot and violent western El Salvador. One day, Wendy and some kids were playing during break and Wendy hit one of the other girls, a silly, childish fight, but a blow that drew blood. When the mother of the girl Wendy hit got to the school, she flew into a rage. She threatened the teacher, the headmaster and Wendy. She told the little girl that she would kill her and her mother. The woman was a member of the Hollywood Locos Salvatrucha gang, an important cell of the Mara Salvatrucha

13. No one reported the incident. Wendy's mother hoped the issue would go no further than these shouted threats, but no. The next week, two gang members stopped her as she was dropping Wendy off at school and told her that she had a debt with the Mara Salvatrucha 13, a debt that would soon be called in. And so it was. They intercepted Wendy's father, Marlon, on his way home from work. They told him the same thing, that he had a debt with the Mara Salvatrucha 13 and they wanted fifty dollars a week. Marlon worked as an accountant for Pepsi and his salary afforded his family a decent lifestyle and even some luxuries, such as taking trips or buying new clothes every once in a while, but fifty dollars a week was beyond his means. He told them he wouldn't pay them a single dollar. The next week the gang got serious. Two gunmen showed up at their house and tried to take Marlon. He managed to close a metal door in time and survive the ambush. They left the next day. The trip to the United States would have been very long and they didn't want to subject Wendy to that. Also, Doris, Wendy's grandmother, wouldn't have survived so many hours walking through the desert. Waiting to see what would happen was not an option. They went to the police and tried to file a report. An officer began to take their statement, but he stopped them as soon as they mentioned the Mara Salvatrucha 13. He told them there was nothing the police could do. That it would be better for them to just leave. Someone recommended they try their luck in Belize, saying they could earn a decent living there and most importantly that the country had one amazing characteristic, something Marlon and María, and not even Wendy, could believe: it was free of gangs.

·   ·   ·

José, deep in concentration, stares out over the turquoise blue of the Atlantic Ocean from one of the short wooden docks on Caulker Island. It's a tiny strip of white sand that survives in the middle of the Caribbean Sea thanks to a formidable coral reef that protects it from waves and the fury of ocean storms. This reef, and the thousands of animals that live on it, fills Caulker Island with tourists from around the world. There are many hotels and bars, and the local islanders sell tours to the German, French, Spanish, and especially US travellers who come to marvel at the vibrant marine life on the reef. Like everyone, José left El Salvador to escape the violence. He wants to live in a place where his kids can grow up without fear and where MS-13 and B-18 are just letters and numbers with no special significance. His story is that of the majority of people here. Whether they came to Belize in the midst of the political–military conflict or to escape the current gang violence, they came because they didn't want to fight. Farmers, business owners, service providers. Peaceful people who don't understand the allure of weapons.

'I won't go back to El Salvador. The MS won't let you live. You have to be careful whenever you go into a new neighbourhood. If they want they'll just stop you and ask for your ID and if they don't like where you come from they'll kill you right there. No. I won't go back to El Salvador. It's better here, it's peaceful here,' says José. And his gaze is once again lost to the infinite blue of the Belizean Caribbean. The land of milk, honey and sea, for Salvadorans who don't want to fight.

NOUR'S EYES

AMANDA MICHALOPOULOU

Translated from the Greek by Patricia Felisa Barbeito

AMANDA MICHALOPOULOU, born in Athens in 1966, is the author of seven novels and three short-story collections. She is a contributing editor of *Kathimerini* in Athens and the *Tagesspiegel* in Berlin. She has been awarded the International Literature Prize by the National Endowment for the Arts (USA) and the Liberis Liber Prize of the Independent Catalan Publishers for her book *I'd Like* (published in English in 2008 by Dalkey Archive Press), as well as the Academy of Athens Prize for her short story collection *Lamperi Mera* [*Bright Day*] (2013). Her novel *Why I Killed My Best Friend* was published in English by Open Letter in 2014, and her stories and essays have been translated into fourteen languages.

PATRICIA FELISA BARBEITO has a Ph.D. in Comparative Literature from Harvard University. She is Professor of American Literatures at the Rhode Island School of Design and a translator of Greek fiction and poetry. Her translations include Menis Koumandareas's *Their Smell Makes Me Want to Cry* (Birmingham Modern Greek Translations, 2004); and Elias Maglinis's *The Interrogation* (Birmingham Modern Greek Translations, 2013) for which she received the 2013 Modern Greek Studies Association's Constantinides Memorial Translation Prize and was shortlisted for the 2014 Greek National Translation Award.

I T was an idyllic trip. We stopped in Trikala for ouzo with a side of *patsa* – tripe soup. It had been a long drive to Epirus, and as the numbness slowly left our limbs, the mythic Greece of my imagination came to life before me: shady paths, rivers, clarinets, arched bridges and locals surprising us with treats of sweetbreads.

Cloaked in the glow of August holidays, my husband, our daughter and I finally arrived at our picturesque hotel on Ioannina lake. That first night, we strolled through Ioannina Castle, the city's historic centre built under the Emperor Justinian. Random snippets from my history book about Ioannina's fortified city popped into my head. I wanted to tell them that Ali Pasha, the fiery and ambitious Ottoman Albanian who took command after the Venetians, had built the walls and the moat. But I stopped myself before opening my mouth. Our daughter is a teenager and she files this type of story under the category of 'Mother's drivel'.

As I walked, I forgot (or tried to forget) that I was in Ioannina to visit a Syrian refugee camp. It was located outside the city, at Katsikas, in a former military airport. In April 2016, after the evacuation of Idomeni, 1,200 refugees had flocked there; 550 remained. Most of them had wanted to leave before they'd even got off the buses that transported them there. They were asking for what newspapers like to call 'stable shelters', but what in everyday language is called a 'home'.

I had never been to a camp before. In my mind's eye, all I could see were photographs in newspapers and footage from news stories on television. Only once, in Athens' Victoria

Square, had I stumbled upon a makeshift shelter for Syrians and Afghans, and it had happened completely by chance. Of course, I'd run into refugees all the time in the city, but they were always in small groups: mothers and their children on the metro, or young men crouching in the middle of a pavement. Moreover, I wasn't visiting the camp in the role of volunteer, but rather as an onlooker charged with writing this essay. Not only did I sense myself floundering at the challenges this would entail, but I was acutely aware of the dissonance of my position: how was I to turn the spotlight on others without turning it on myself? Before I'd even set foot in the camp, I felt like an intruder.

Somehow, I had to lay bare my own vulnerabilities. The first step was to try to understand why I had accepted this assignment – what did I hope to accomplish? I'd been involved in the refugee issue chiefly as a spectator. Refugeehood was a spectacle in the sense that it made me think of the term 'poor-nography' coined by the curator Tirdad Zolghadr to describe the voyeuristic use of images of extreme poverty and precarity in the media and the arts – a fetishistic impulse veiled as human interest. As a Greek woman, a citizen of a country that hosted thousands of refugees, I also felt implicated by circumstances. I was extremely saddened by everything I saw. It struck me that the refugee situation was disturbing not only for the obvious humanitarian reasons, but because it touched on something more selfish: it triggered a strange form of identification; the deep well of fear plumbed by coming face to face with what it means to be forced to abandon one's home, to be torn away from one's heritage, to find one's existence razed to the ground, to be completely uprooted.

All the while, I was confronted with smooth-talking report-ers on television who, due to either discomfort or inexperience, turned the refugees into a homogeneous mass of pain. Like latter-day Robespierres, they transformed commiseration into political virtue for the enlightened television watchers as they contemplated the benighted refugees. It's all so neat: human pain becomes the means for abstract moral judgement, as Hannah Arendt would say. André Malraux, of course, put it even more succinctly: 'I don't like a humanity derived from the contemplation of suffering.'

For me, the challenge was to maintain an equilibrium. I did not want to remain cold and detached, eager to discern manipulation, self-interest and simplification wherever I turned. On the other hand, I also did not want to find myself accidentally tearing up behind my black sunglasses.

In her email message, Karen had sent me detailed instructions: 'Take the road that goes through Anatoli and continues on to Katsikas. As you drive out of the village, you'll see a petrol station on your left; soon after that you'll come upon some old military warehouses on your right. Take the narrow road to the camp's car park. Also, please don't wear nice clothes, and cover your shoulders and knees. I cannot promise that you'll get in, because you'll have to show your ID and since it's Greek they may realise that you don't belong to an organisation. Normally, only those who have received permission from the Ministry of the Interior are allowed entry.'

I was dismayed. I didn't have time for official permits. My only plan was to show up by myself and see what happened. The fine point about covering my shoulders in the middle of August baffled me: I had packed only strappy tops. I was even more disconcerted by the tenor of the instructions. Why was I being told how to dress? What was this about? Finally, after much looking around, I found a minidress to pair with my jeans. When I walked out of the hotel's air-conditioned reception area into the street, I thought I would faint. Don't be such a drama queen, I said to myself. Is it that difficult to comply with others' wishes?

My greatest fear on the way there was emotional dishonesty. What exactly was I planning to do at the camp? Observe these strangers and their powerful stories? There is no training or experience that prepares us for this type of encounter. What are you supposed to do exactly? Do you simply walk up to people and ask them about their lives? Or – and this is much worse – do you go prepared to pity them? I was disturbed by the orchestrated predisposition to pity: the surging of that shallow, televised 'feel-good' emotion that requires people to be viewed not as individuals but as a homogeneous mass, hungry for mercy and comfort. Pity makes you feel like a good person, a superior person. Pity, just like guilt, separates people into victims and victimisers.

I wanted to be natural and forthright, but it was incredibly difficult. What I encountered was an enormous photograph: scenes that I'd become familiar with on the news during the preceding months now spread out before me. A cluster of military vehicles decked with the Red Cross symbol were parked at the entrance to the camp. Now there was no room for fanciful interpretation or misunderstanding, only stifling heat, pebbles under children's running feet and sand spinning in the air.

Karen was helping to interpret for a sick child and could not meet with me right away. I handed over my ID – no one questioned me about anything – and started wandering around. The first buildings I encountered were the storehouses. Roofs of nickel sheeting and wooden frames holding row upon row of shelving for supplies. 'This is a shop, not a store cupboard,' I read. Later, I found out that the refugees had to make an appointment to visit the shop. This was essential – otherwise there would be mayhem. Volunteers, young and old, from Spain and the US, were moving chairs. A young Syrian was stitching together colourful scraps of cloth on a sewing machine. A group of children lay on a rug, busily colouring in Disney princesses in their sketch books. The legs of stuffed animals, baby nappies, canned goods, bundles of clothes, well-worn shoes and men's belts poked out from the surrounding cardboard boxes.

I walked out and sat in the shade by the entrance, on the only bench. A woman was standing next to me, talking loudly with a young soldier, like the people on news reports. 'Ever since these poor people arrived here, I cannot sleep. Do you understand? I feel a heavy weight pressing down on my heart all day. How is it possible that something like this can happen?' She kept slapping her hands on her knees, as if she were keening. Next to her a young Syrian held out a mobile phone to those around him: 'My home,' he said, and I craned my neck to get a look. It was a ruin, all mud and beams.

I thought of William Carlos Williams's poem 'The House', the poetic counterpart to Emmanuel Levinas's views on hospitality. When I was younger, I'd wanted to put it up outside the door to my dorm room, a reminder of both generosity and humility. I'd learnt it off by heart:

> *The house is yours*
> *To wander in as you please –*
> *Your breakfast will be kept*
> *Ready for you until*

You choose to arise!
This is the front door
Where we stood penniless
by the hogshead of crockery.

This is the kitchen –
We have a new hot-water heater and a new
gas stove to please you

The poem ends like this:

The whole house
Is waiting for you
To walk in it at your pleasure
It is yours.

I did not know who the house in front of me belonged to. This camp trembling in the heat; this cloudy, ramshackle village; this neighbourhood of shadows, one next to the other, and full of persecuted people about whom I knew nothing besides the clichéd snapshot of their lives. Their individual stories were now crowded together in tents under heat that was forty degrees in the shade, if there was any shade to be had, that is. There wasn't a tree in sight. In front of the bathrooms with their solar water heaters, mothers washed children or clothes in tubs. Men walked together in twos. The front row of tents was flanked by improvised gardens full of every possible crop: lettuce, tomato, onions – they were the only residents who had dared, quite literally, to take root here.

Out of nowhere, a girl with sparkling black eyes appeared. Smiling, she sat down next to me and stared with unabashed curiosity while her mother chatted in Arabic to some people

I couldn't see. I found the girl's intensity captivating. When she started speaking to me in English in her high, ringing voice, I started to feel more comfortable. Our conversation flowed naturally.

Nour was twelve years old. On her small, old-fashioned mobile phone, she showed me pixelated pictures of her siblings, then tapped in my number so that we might make arrangements to meet again. In her broken but expressive English she told me about how they had been smuggled out of Syria through the borders to Israel. 'So big waves, look,' she said and raised her hand up to the sky. 'Very difficult, people sick.' Then, looking down at her shoes, 'They took very much money.'

Nour said that she really wanted a hat and sunglasses, and impulsively I reached up to give her mine. I had forgotten that my sunglasses came with lenses for short-sightedness.

'Want me to send you a pair of sunglasses?'

'Oh, we don't live here any more. We live in a regular house. That man over there will take us with his lorry. I don't know the address. We're here to visit the rest of the family and some of our friends.'

'What was it like here?'

'It was fine.'

'What about where you are now?'

'It's better.'

They were in a hurry to leave and the girl was holding them back. Someone honked the lorry's horn.

When she'd crossed the road and was about to get into the lorry, she turned to look at me. 'My name means something like your Greek name Foteini, full of light.'

I should have known: she sparkled.

.   .   .

Karen teaches comparative literature at Princeton. She'd brought eight students who were interested in helping to Katsikas. Two of them speak Farsi and are much in demand, even though not many Afghans remain in the camp because of tensions with the Syrians. Karen has already travelled twice to Idomeni; she has contributed greatly to the refugee effort, but she does not want me to write about this. She wants this part of her work to remain invisible. I can at least say that she is the translator of my books in the US. That she is an extraordinarily sensitive and generous woman who loves literature and people. That we started off as collaborators and ended up as friends. Now, as we walked under the searing sun, we disagreed about the instructions on how to dress.

'Look at it this way,' Karen said. 'This is their home. And at home they ought to do whatever they want and be in an environment where they feel comfortable.'

'But I too want to be comfortable.'

'Yes, but you are entering their home.'

The house is yours – the poem popped into my mind again. 'But this is not a home. it's a ghetto, a type of limbo.'

'This camp is a temporary home. It's an issue of respect for their customs. When they go to the village, they see how people dress over here. And if they end up living here they will have to adapt and learn how things work.'

I don't know if she is right. Most problems are caused by the inability to adapt. The trick for the expatriate is what Tzvetan Todorov describes as the imperative not to confuse the real with the ideal, culture with nature. I know this trick, because it was something that I too struggled with during the seven years that I lived in Berlin. I know some people will object to the comparison: it's one thing to emigrate and another thing entirely to be a refugee. Yet in both cases, one's identity is at stake. Anyone who is expatriated shares a sadness, a sense of bereavement. At the same time, you are granted the ability to start entirely anew, as Todorov, from personal experience, writes: 'There is no drama for the individual in the loss of a culture, on condition that he acquires another.'

Before Karen arrived to pick me up, I felt like an intruder and I didn't know what to do. I walked between the rows of tents with my arms folded behind my back, like a nineteenth-century explorer. As if strolling through this strange, unnatural place was completely natural; as if the place itself had become completely normal given the lack of another viable or better alternative.

Awkwardly, I kept walking and peering through the tents' openings, at a crouching woman cooking here, at two crawling children there. At some point, I spied a detergent that is no longer on the market but that I remembered from childhood. The women's movements reminded me of the way I used to play with my little pots and pans as a child; how I would arrange pine needles, corks and firethorn berries on top of a low, cement-block wall for my cooking. Now, I found myself playing Homo Faber, he who derives judgement from contemplation. And there, across from me, was Homo Ludens, he who continues playing, even in the midst of tragedy.

Karen then appeared and delivered me from my awkwardness and bizarre stream of thoughts. She took me to a tent where, later that afternoon, a computer class for women aged between sixteen and eighty was due to take place. We walked through another tent: about twenty primary-school-aged children were watching an animated movie, *Frozen*. A little boy began hitting his neighbour, sneakily, then he turned on the other boys. The volunteers tried to pry them apart, but the little boy kept raining blows blindly into the air. It was clear that he was fighting something else, something weighty and symbolic that had not yet been given a name. The girls sat quietly in the front row, hypnotised by the colourful images.

We made our way to the big tent dedicated to recreation and entertainment. It was the middle of the afternoon and a deathly silence reigned. This tent was made of thicker fabric and there were places where you could stand without becoming covered in sweat. Under the centre stanchion a group of children were playing chess with volunteers from Lighthouse Relief, the group which the students from Princeton had joined. I sat on a kilim, next to a student who was lying down. She had a pleasant warmth in her eyes. She spoke to me of the first days that her group had spent on Lesvos cleaning the beaches. Of all the waste, what had most remained with her were the battered Styrofoam life-savers that the smugglers used and the deflated children's floaties. She said: 'We're leaving in September, but over here everything will remain the same.'

Not exactly. As I write these lines at the end of the summer, tensions are on the rise again in Katsikas. Some families are leaving the camp and erecting their tents in the middle of the village in protest. They were promised that they'd be moved to Athens, but nothing has come of it. Via Skype, Karen tells me: 'They've been duped. From the beginning, this camp was built on lies.' She tells me what happened in the weeks following my visit: 'I went to Idomeni again. I wanted to see what had remained of the camp. There was only one Isobox structure and one tent. They had thrown all the garbage in the gulch behind the camp, even the tents. The senseless waste is mind-boggling. Back then we were begging for tents; we erected Isoboxes that cost five thousand euros each, and for what? The country just cannot accept that some of the refugees will remain here and that they need real homes. Instead, all they're offering is temporary solutions for a permanent problem.'

I returned to my hotel that afternoon. The reception, icy with air conditioning and impersonality, was in complete counterpoint to all that I had witnessed that day. It reminded me of the famous 'Hotelhalle' (Hotel Lobby) by Siegfried Kracauer: 'It is a coming and going of unknowns who are changed into empty forms by forgetting their passwords, and who parade, imperceptible, like Chinese shadows. If they had an interiority, it would have no windows.'

In our room, my loved ones were sleeping. They looked so peaceful, so safe. It was my turn now to find myself in an interiority without windows: in a well-appointed hotel room, from which I could order a club sandwich. I felt like an amateur dramatics actor who has two roles in the same performance and isn't convincing in either of them. This numbness lasted two days. I returned to my life. The only things that remained to remind me of Katsikas were my notes and a selfie I'd taken with Nour.

After Epirus, we went to Donoussa, an island in the Cyclades, accompanied by friends from Berlin. One day, while our daughters went diving off the pier, Barbara and I decided to head towards the camping area. We climbed uphill from Pera Panta and took the path that leads to Kedros. I wanted to show my friend this beautiful beach with the sunken hull of a German raider, left over from the Second World War. Then, after we'd gone swimming and finished our fruit juices, we walked to the tents behind the restaurant. As soon as I set eyes on them, I was immediately transported back to Katsikas. There were the tents again, arranged neatly in rows, flanked by lines with hanging clothes. The only things that betrayed the fact that tourists were staying in them were a man wearing a straw hat and a few tamarisk shrubs in the background. The sunken ship was also at fault for it had rekindled so many memories: rescue teams, Europol, European disputes about how best to protect the Greek coastline, and the deflated children's floaties the students had told me about.

'What's wrong?' Barbara asked.

We talked about how difficult it is today to separate reality from representation. You could even go so far as to say that the unwashed tourist who grows a beard while on his wanderings imitates the refugee. He's playing a safe game of nomadism. A photographer friend of mine took a picture of the crowds of people at the Thirassia volcano near Santorini, a long, undulating queue. 'Refugees?' I asked. 'No, tourists.'

A little before I finished this essay, an architect friend lent me Francesco Carreri's book *Walkscapes: Walking as an Aesthetic Practice*. There I found the phrase that untied the knot and reconciled me with the piece I was writing, with the fact that I was writing it without having reached any definitive conclusions:

> Nomadic transhumance, generally thought of as the archetype for any journey, was actually the development of the endless wanderings of hunters in the Palaeolithic period, whose symbolic meanings were translated by the Egyptians in the *ka*, the symbol of 'eternal wandering'. This primitive roving lived on in religion (the journey as ritual) and in literary forms (the journey as narrative).

The journey as narrative; movement as both literal and meta-phorical; the hieroglyphic *ka*, representing in its two outspread arms the divine grace enveloping anyone who travels the world. Everything demanded that I feel the mystery of these corre-lations: tents languishing at the mercy of the sun; volunteers travelling from every corner of the world; and I, who found myself there, not-so-accidentally. But more than anything, Nour's eyes.

In the meantime, Nour has returned to Katsikas. She writes to me on WhatsApp and tells me her news: 'Today it's raining at the camp', or 'I don't know if I will go to school' – stuff like that – and I regale her with useless adult advice that she doesn't need, because it's perfectly clear she will find her own way. I believe in Nour's individuality; I believe in her capability, it's apparent in her eyes. When I think of her, I don't think of her as a Syrian refugee, she doesn't need that label. I think of her simply as an extraordinary, radiant little girl.

LAND OF HEROES

LITHUANIA'S VERY OWN
REFUGEE CRISIS

NILS MOHL

Translated from the German by Max Reinhold

Author NILS MOHL published his debut novel *Kasse 53* [Cash Register 53] in 2008, followed by his collection of short stories *Ich wäre tendenziell für ein Happy End* [I Tend to Prefer a Happy Ending] in 2009, and four more novels. *Es war einmal Indianerland* [Once Upon an Indian Land] won the Jugendliteraturpreis (YA Literature Award) in 2012. He has received several other awards for his literary work, including the Literary Award of the City of Hamburg and the Oldenburg Children and YA Literature Prize.

MAX REINHOLD is an itinerant journeyman in the fields of fiction and non-fiction. For many years he has gladly served the work of Nils Mohl whenever the occasion has arisen.

THE shutters just won't stop. All lenses are trained on the athletic young man who would fit right in in a soap opera, playing the boy next door. If pubescent girls had a poster of him above their beds, no parents would lose sleep. Wavy hair, cheeky looks, and as clean-shaven as in an aftershave commercial; he is wearing a down jacket with fur hood and carrying a backpack. One might suspect the twenty-five-year-old is on his way to attend a postgrad lecture. In fact, a pack of media representatives are blocking his way at Vilnius airport. They want him to comment.

Wednesday, 6 April 2016. A scene so often seen: the star arrives. The story will be reported in the evening news. Every child will hear his name: Basir Yousofy. He jovially declares there is no place he'd rather be at the moment, not even Germany. Though he's heard they are quite wealthy over there, Lithuania is his first choice. He wants to stay, he says. And he says it in Lithuanian.

Basir is a refugee from Afghanistan.

About the same time a young man in Greece still dreams of Ireland. He has contacts there, speaks English with a slight British accent – which he has purposefully acquired on his own. His name: Redwan Eid. He attended Al Furat University in Syria. Later, he was a journalist in Damascus, working for newspapers and radio stations. But he is made for the screen. His jaw-length hair is slicked back, his chin sexy with stubble. He'd look good modelling suits. In everyday life, however, he prefers shorts and a T-shirt. He has headphones of the brand Beats by Dr. Dre around his neck.

Redwan is a refugee as well and places his hopes in the new EU relocation programme. On the application he is allowed to name six countries he favours and even to prioritise them. Then he waits. May comes and he celebrates his thirty-fourth birthday abroad. Finally the call comes. He asks if Ireland will be possible, but he is not given any info via the phone. EASO, the European Asylum Support Office, asks him to visit their Athens bureau.

The woman behind the desk is a blonde, barely thirty: Tanya. She plays with her hair. Redwan forces a sarcastic smile. 'Lithuania? Do they speak any English there at all?' The only thing he knows for sure about the country: he has not named it on his list. Tanya still curls her hair. She explains the wish list is exactly that: a wish list. The fine print, she says, explains all this.

Redwan closes his eyes. The very first story he published as a journalist was a parody. The candidates of a fictitious talent show got humiliated, victims of their own gullibility. He never would have believed reality could top it. Lithuania?

The map of the world shows Denmark and Switzerland being considerably smaller. Lithuania does not suffer from lack of space. There are only 2.8 million residents in an area which is a little smaller than Bavaria but three times the size of Israel. As a comparison, 12 million people live in Bavaria, in Israel more than 8 million.

The majority of Lithuanians are Catholic. And basketball fans. Basketball is the national pastime. Malicious tongues add: besides booze and suicide. Truth is, the biggest Lithuanian hero nowadays is Arvydas Sabonis, who made it to the NBA. At the 1992 Barcelona Olympic Games he led the Lithuanian team to the bronze medal – the first Olympic Games after the independence of the country. Basketball courts litter Lithuania.

Another truth: according to the last report of the WHO, about thirty per cent of all deaths in Lithuania are alcohol related. And another part of the picture is that Lithuania has held a European record for years: statistically about three people commit suicide there every day. Nowhere on the continent is the rate higher.

Winters are cold, dark and long. Spring only really arrives in May. In summer, however, the beaches of the Baltic Sea are very inviting. The local currency is the euro – Lithuania has been an EU member for more than twelve years. About twenty-five years ago, in a daze of happiness, the country achieved independence from the Soviet Union... but neighbouring Russia still looms large. In the course of the twentieth century, Poland and Germany were occupying forces as well. As early as the 1920s, during the first independence, the geographer Kazys Pakštas devised plans to relocate the population in the case of imminent invasion. To evacuate the entire population – to Venezuela, Madagascar or straight to the Bahamas. Pakštas was occasionally likened to Abraham Lincoln and Alexander von Humboldt. Lithuanians are historically sensitive to foreign threats, real and perceived, the country being in a political cauldron, geographically speaking.

Ever since the influx of refugees to Europe increased considerably last year, the Lithuanian public has argued about the immigration of aliens with new ardour. The German Goethe Institute in Vilnius posed a debate question for students this spring: 'Should Lithuania proactively court refugees?' It was a deliberate provocation. The culture of the Baltic state seems as far from welcoming as the Baltic Sea is from the Hindu Kush.

Though the Lithuanian government had, in September 2015, as part of the EU relocation programme, committed to admitting 1,105 refugees from Greece and Italy within the following two years, by July 2016 only twenty-nine had arrived. Politicians sure didn't force the matter. In the autumn there will be elections.

Inquiries to the Vilnius branch of the UNHCR elicit the explanation that there is insufficient infrastructure for the integration of refugees. Only two state-run institutions for housing asylum seekers and refugees exist: in Rukla and Pabradė, two towns barely findable on a map.

Lithuania. Really? Tanya in the Athens office of the EASO nods and hands Redwan a form, printed in Greek characters. He has ten minutes to think it over. Redwan wants to throw a fit, feels like crying. Tanya wants him to sign. Redwan yells, but cuts out the crying. This document in front of him determines his future and he can't even read it? He jumps up from his chair, wants to leave the room. But then what? The odyssey of recent months, the red tape, the waiting have worn on him. Eventually he sits down and picks up the pen. That's it. Signed. Sealed. He asks for a copy but Tanya shakes her head. No copy. But soon he will have an appointment at the Lithuanian embassy.

At this point, two years have passed since the day Redwan decides to leave Damascus. He loves his fatherland as much as he hates President Bashar Hafiz al-Assad – and he makes no bones about it. When he lies in bed at night and hears a car stop in the street, the slamming of doors, steps approaching, he always expects it to be the henchmen of the regime coming for him. In September 2014, he finally gives in to the urgings of his mother and sisters.

The first station in his wanderings is Mersin, a booming town in Turkey, where he teaches English to Syrian countrymen in a private school. Next stop is Istanbul. Here he works as a broadcaster for a radio station run by exiles. Meanwhile, Redwan's brother has made it to Munich. They talk on the phone. Who knows how things will go in Turkey? Intense negotiations between Ankara and the EU about the refugee crisis are ongoing. And the situation in Syria remains disastrous, no silver lining in sight. To apply for asylum in Europe seems to be the most reasonable thing to do now.

The regular ferry from Izmir takes about twenty minutes to cover the five miles and a ticket is twenty euros. The smugglers take 600 dollars for the trip to Greece – life vests are available for a surcharge. The inflatable raft is discoloured, the material looks brittle. Redwan can't swim. But that night, being on the water, he has minutes of inner peace. What more is there to lose now? The coastguard intercepts the vessel with forty refugees after about an hour and ships them to the island of Chios.

This is what Redwan explains in his interview at the embassy. An envoy of the state department, flown in from Vilnius, asks questions. Redwan's answers seem to be satisfactory and he receives assurance that his prospects are excellent, not least because of his language skills. There are hints that contacts with the media and prospective employers already exist and he is clued in on why he is so welcome: he is educated, presentable, young, ambitious. This is exactly what Redwan hated in Syria, even before the civil war, the nepotism. Is the whole world nothing but a battlefield or a rigged talent show?

At last Redwan wearily asks where he will be placed. Rukla, they tell him. Back in the hotel he looks up the town on Google. The search engine shows tanks and soldiers.

.   .   .

The first Lithuanian armed forces Basir saw were real: a 200-strong reconstruction team had moved out to Afghanistan in 2005. Part of ISAF (NATO's International Security Assistance Force), it takes the helm in Ghor province. Basir is still a teenager. The only Lithuanian casualty during eight years of deployment in the Hindu Kush will be one officer.

About three years later, in March 2016, the freelance journalist Josh Friedman wanders the refugee camp at Idomeni near the Greek–Macedonian border. Thousands of people are stranded there after the closing of the route over the Balkans. Friedman, just twenty-six, gangly and with a crew cut, grew up in California but has been living for some time in Bulgaria's capital, Sofia, using it as his base to tour Europe in his quest for exclusive news. There are rumours the camp is about to be closed. Turkey and the EU have just inked their refugee deal.

Friedman is recording sound bites at a food counter when a man his age asks for help. It is Basir, who tells him he worked for the Lithuanian troops in Afghanistan as an interpreter. After their withdrawal the Taliban sent him death threats, he says. He carries them with him.

He also shows Friedman photos of himself with ISAF soldiers. Friedman hears the sound of tent fabric flapping in the spring breeze. He looks over the garbage-strewn moonscape, border fences lining the horizon. He is aware that virtually every person there would be prepared to invent something to escape the misery of this dead end. But somebody insisting on getting to Lithuania is patently bizarre. It is 20 March 2016. Friedman offers to record an interview with Basir in English and a video message in Lithuanian. He says he can't promise anything, but if what Basir says holds water – he is very well connected.

'*Laba diena visiems iš Lietuvos,*' Basir says, looking into the camera unshaven. 'A nice day to all people in Lithuania.' Basir asks the people of Lithuania and their president for help and ends his statement with the words: 'I love Lithuania. Thank you very much. Goodbye.'

Eleven days later. Friedman is back in Sofia and has subtitled the thirty-three-second video. He uploads it. An hour or so later the first TV stations in Lithuania commence reporting. Commander Jurgis Norvaisa, who served in Afghanistan, tells the public that he knows Basir. The case gains more and more momentum: representatives of the Lithuanian government contact the refugee via his Facebook page; international media pick up the story.

In a matter of days, Basir is issued the required visas. He is in Athens now, sleeping in a hotel bed. There is time for a shave and some shopping. He wants to build something in Lithuania. He thinks of opening a restaurant. Less than a week after Friedman has uploaded the video, Basir's plane lands in Vilnius. He hopes to be reunited with his two-year-old daughter and his family soon.

A picture of everyday life in Vilnius: a covered market on the edge of the old town. Not far from it a group of impoverished people have taken over part of the street. An elderly lady is sitting on a plastic bucket, selling carrots. Another one offers cut flowers. A third one uses a cardboard box as a table for apples, as puny as a child's fist. The next one offers nylon stockings.

The façade behind them is emblazoned with the glaring sign of the supermarket chain Maxima, the top dog with more than 230 branches all over the country. The main shareholder is Nerijus Numavičius, son of a chauffeur and a teacher. A fairy-tale story – the forty-nine-year-old is the only Lithuanian billionaire.

The upheavals after the demise of socialism generated winners and losers. Wealth is increasing, but the rising tide does not lift all boats. Even though the rate of unemployment is 9 per cent and thus about average for the EU, one in three Lithuanians lives in poverty and is far, very far away from carefree shopping at Maxima.

Which brings us to the big migrant problem of Lithuania, the real one: droves of Lithuanians leave the country, young ones in particular. The emigration number fluctuates between thirty and forty thousand individuals per year: craftspeople, doctors, teachers, college students. Name the fifth biggest city of Lithuanians these days? London. Calculated by the number of residents with Lithuanian passports or origins, more than 100,000 migrants from Lithuania live by the Thames.

Almost every single family in the country has members who have tried their luck abroad – in Western Europe, Canada, New Zealand. Shouldn't this be conducive to an understanding of the plight of uprooted humans? Anyway: Why isn't the current worldwide political situation actually seen as an opportunity? The emigration haemorrhage of recent years leaves a shrinking and ageing population. Doesn't Lithuania in fact need many more refugees than just a couple of dozen or hundred?

If the problem were left to market forces, at least 20,000 would come tomorrow, according to Karolis Žibas, a sociologist from the Centre for Ethnic Studies in Vilnius, who is convinced of this. But he adds that the Lithuanian mindset is not even remotely ready for such an influx.

By which he means there is a lack of tolerance towards minorities, regardless of whether they're LGBT people, immigrants or of a different faith. Because, among other reasons, Lithuanians simply have no relevant experience. Refugees used to be politically persecuted people from Russia, Belarus and Ukraine. Not more than a couple of hundred per year. The obstacles to integration in terms of language, ethnicity and religion were low.

This is the missing part of the picture: even in Vilnius it's rare to see people of colour, except for tourists. International conglomerates erect steel and glass towers, as they do everywhere, and blanket the best locations in the shopping areas with their stores. But there are no Mediterranean delis, Pakistani cab drivers, African restaurants or Asian nail salons.

Redwan flies on 20 June 2016. In an ironic aside his stopover is Istanbul. It is the day of his father's death. He orders a drink in the airport café. Later he won't remember if it was coffee or a Coke. He exchanges messages with friends in town, coming close to skedaddling, to once again going into hiding in Turkey. But he recognises that for the first time since he left Syria everything is in legal order, more or less. Still, what is the trade-off? Family, home, job – lost. Though a new chapter of his life is about to commence, this revelation hits him in the gut and overwhelms him: he starts crying and slowly makes his way back to the gate.

From Vilnius he is being transferred straight to Rukla. A drive of ninety minutes, through undeveloped landscape, mostly unpopulated with the odd wooden house, brightly painted and with fruit trees in front. Mixed woodland follows, birches and pines, lots of pines. Finally Rukla. The car pulls up in front of a renovated prefab building at the end of a street with many more prefab buildings, barracks of the Lithuanian armed forces.

Redwan arrives in the evening, though dusk just won't fall. Add deep silence – there is no sound from anywhere. He puts on his headphones, listens to Arab music, puts away his luggage. His entire library consists of the fifteen books he places on veneer shelves. There is the *Oxford Dictionary*, more English dictionaries and *The Last of the Mohicans*. Which is what he feels like. And is to his liking: in the refugee block he will prefer to be left alone in the coming weeks.

He writes an article about his escape for 'DELFI', the internet portal of the *Lithuanian Tribune*. Another item on his schedule is language lessons, conducted by an old schoolteacher who does the chalk and talk, devoid of humour, using material for primary-school education. She fills the blackboard with handwriting, conjugating verbs. Bemusement fills the room. Not everybody in the group even knows the Latin characters. And the language itself is full of obstacles, with seven cases, excessive use of diminutives and odd inflections. A single adjective can take on up to 150 forms. Is Redwan really supposed to cram all this?

In fact he lands a job without the language, working for Western Union in Vilnius. They gladly take him, first as a paid apprentice, being trained in customer service. He is to communicate with clients from the Arab region. He would never have imagined ending up in finance one day. But this way he gets out of Rukla. A magnanimous Lithuanian grants him temporary shelter in her house. Finding an apartment on his own proves difficult: landlords do not seem keen to rent to a single Syrian man. Redwan's ad on a Facebook list is deleted immediately.

August comes to an end, the days shorten. Lithuania it is. Redwan has to stay for at least four years, or else he risks losing his status as an approved refugee. Only after four years will he be allowed to choose his place of residence and work within the EU somewhere of his own volition. This is the ruling of the EU relocation programme and what the European laws for asylum determine.

In September, Redwan posts on Facebook that exile makes him feel like the walking dead. It is the second anniversary of his farewell from Syria. He writes, 'From time to time I find myself in another graveyard, that's all'.

And at the moment that's Lithuania.

Vilnius hipsters look somehow more bearded, pierced and tattooed than their brethren in Leipzig, Stockholm, Helsinki. The wardrobe and make-up of young women make it seem like it's always Friday night. Being overweight is not a widespread problem for either sex.

There is a theory that societies that emerged from the stranglehold of the Soviet Union were at first especially keen on adopting Western European habits and standards. A kind of mimicry, mainly in the areas of fashion, music and leisure activities.

Lithuania is twenty-six, a young nation, and seems in many aspects as insecure as a person of that age, looking for an identity, a future, a place in life. Maybe one day history books will tell that the worldwide refugee crisis at the beginning of the twenty-first century was a time of inner growth for Lithuania, a test and a stepping stone on the way to finding itself. Don't we wish this for the whole of Europe?

Today we can say for sure that Europeans have been fortunate to realise that Europe is something that concerns all of us, all of us who are a part of it. Which includes Lithuanians. This is a blessing. Everything else will take years, if not generations. What will happen to Basir is an open question, even though he was welcomed to the country like a movie star and everybody I talked to in August 2016 knew of him and the circumstances of his arrival. What will happen to his daughter? What will happen to the children who will be born here as the children of refugees? Will they become legends in the future, win the first gold medal in basketball for Lithuania?

I've spoken to activists who collect donated clothing for people in refugee shelters, who act as interlocutors, who stage theatre projects, who help to build bridges between aliens and locals. I've seen the member of a human rights organisation cry when she told me of her experiences in the Foreigners' Registration Centre in Pabradė. She struggled to change the officials' attitude – that it's not the protection from, but the protection of, refugees that should govern their actions.

I've met Redwan Eid in Rukla, I've taken an evening walk with him, strolling through the old town of Vilnius and learning that the cobblestones there can remind you of Damascus. I've thought a lot about what one might ignore by seeing things through the slightly arrogant eyes of an outsider, as a German. The year 2016 is, for Lithuanians, as far away from (or close to) independence as Germany was from the end of the Second World War in 1971. Back then strangers were still quite strange to us too.

EPILOGUE

One more truth: there are exactly two state-run institutions devoted to the housing of asylum seekers and refugees in

Lithuania, Rukla und Pabradė. There is a documentary about these places, *Almost Sweden* by Audrius Lelkaitis, that is worth watching. Or are they non-places? Pabradė in particular, close to the border of Belarus, suggests such a categorisation.

People who get caught entering Lithuania illegally or those whose asylum application is still being processed end up there, behind the walls of the registration centre, in a renovated prefab. Men, women, children. If the application is denied or asylum not granted the person turns into a detainee in the prison wing nearby, beside those who have been apprehended without papers or who are not seeking asylum in Lithuania because they wish to move on, to some other place.

The documentary shows steel doors, massive bolts and locks, soulless chambers with walls in dreary colours. There is a paved courtyard, an enclosure as gloomy as a zoo. Children play, barbed wire in the background. A guard hits a refugee with his elbow. The head of the institution, Colonel Volikas, appears looking like a movie villain: pale with a short fringe of hair, ginger moustache and pinstripe suit.

Empty of feeling, he explains that currently the situation is so abnormal that the interests of migrants precede those of the country. Asked if his experiences there sometimes touch him, his eyes briefly light up. 'An odd question,' he says. 'How could a surgeon operate if the task hurt his feelings?'

Wednesday, 31 August 2016: on the day of my departure, I drive north-east on a dead straight blacktop, through one of those signature pine forests that gleam in the morning light, red at the bottom and deep green at the top. After travelling half the distance, the vista opens on to pasture and every now and then, seeming out of place in this wasteland, is a crooked house.

After an hour, Pabradė greets me with a radar flash and a campaign poster showing some guy in a suit. A little further on, a petrol station. What did I expect? A monstrous fortress with watchtowers and heavily armed patrols? A symbol of an overextended government, set in stone and barbed wire, eternally anachronistic? Faces in despair, pressed against metal window gratings?

I park the car directly across the street from the refugee institution, on a sandy stretch full of potholes. To my back stand wooden cabins, surrounded by apple trees. So, this is Pabradė? The walls of the compound, decorated with a Soviet-style geometric pattern, are about six feet tall and picturesquely shabby, but overgrown with trees and only one side is crowned with rusty concertina wire. Next door, Maxima is open for business, glass doors shining.

I am in front of an iron gate; next to it is a hut with a wooden door, maybe some sort of gatehouse. The background is deco-rated with flagpoles and a three-storey building, made of grey brick, worn by time and the elements. I take three pictures. What next? I feel like setting off for the airport, though I'm in no hurry. Without a permit there's probably no chance of a tour.

Then suddenly the little door opens. A stocky man in mili-tary trousers and a camouflage T-shirt appears. Bulging biceps, a little paunch, a staunch fourteen stone. An absurdly small peaked cap shades his gruff mug. In combat boots he marches towards me, looking as if his card game has been interrupted at a very inauspicious moment – and I am to blame.

No car in sight. No breeze. Only the crunch of his boots. He barks at me in Lithuanian. When he realises I don't understand he switches to English. He shows a pale-blue plastic ID, level with his belt and gun-filled holster.

'I'm from Border Control. You took pictures.'

'Yes. Just the building.'

'What do you think you're doing here!'

'I'm a writer from Germany.'

'You have to delete the pictures.'

'I don't understand.'

'It's a government building. Show me the pictures.'

He looks at the camera screen, then straight back into my eyes:

'Delete.'

'Why?'

He inhales briskly.

'Because.'

That cheers him up. He wrinkles his nose, which is crooked, the shape betraying that it has been broken at least once.

'Because? That's good,' I say.

'Show me your passport.'

He takes down my particulars, and the car registration.

I throw the camera into the car.

'A rental car?'

'Yes.'

'Where are you going from here?'

'To the airport.'

'Are the photos deleted? Show me the camera.'

I haven't deleted the pictures yet. He immediately grasps that. He wipes his nose with his thumb. I delete them.

'Have a nice trip.'

He disappears back through the door, possibly back to the card game. I stare at the building I am not allowed to take pictures of. And I ask myself: Is that the end of the story? But then the door opens again. A group of people exit, three women with headscarves, two bearded men, four children. They look like extras, costumed refugees. They amble past me, past Maxima, in the direction of the centre of the village. I look at their retreating forms and can't help feeling they have been sent out because of me.

UNDER THE
TOKYO SKYTREE

THE TALE OF A REFUGEE
FROM CONGO

MASATSUGU ONO

Translated from the Japanese by Samuel Malissa

MASATSUGU ONO was born in Japan in 1970 and obtained his Ph.D. in Literature from the University of Paris VIII. His debut novel *Mizu ni Umoreru Haka* [The Water-Covered Grave] won the Asahi New Writers' Award in 2001; his second novel *Nigiyakana wan ni seowareta fune* [Boat on a Choppy Bay] won the Mishima Yukio Award one year later. Ono has published a range of short stories and a further novel, as well as the novella *Kyunen-mae no inori* [A Prayer Nine Years Ago] for which he won the 2014 Akutagawa Prize, and *At The Edge Of The Wood*, published in English by Strangers Press in 2017.

SAMUEL MALISSA translates both fiction and non-fiction from Japanese into English. He is currently a Ph.D. candidate at Yale University.

H E's in the VIP lounge, which is where government people go. That's what his friend told him. Looking around he sees men and women of all different nationalities in folk costumes and well-made suits, relaxing on fine chairs and sofas. It's nicely air-conditioned, far more comfortable than the gate areas for normal people. They're chatting affably, reading newspapers, reading magazines, waiting for their flights. As he sits there in his good suit and pale green shirt, flipping the pages of a magazine, he too could pass for a high-level government official.

But there is an essential difference between him and the others, one that can't be seen. His heart thrums in his chest. The anxiety is crushing. Inside he's screaming, Come on, come on. And even though he keeps it in, he's still afraid someone might hear him.

All he has with him is the small, grey rolling suitcase, there by his feet. It's nearly empty, just one change of clothes: one jacket, one pair of trousers, one pair of underwear. Sandals. Cash. A printout of his hotel reservation. A few books. And his passport… The photograph on the passport is unmistakably him, but the name next to it is not his. It does not say Massamba Mangala.

Come on, hurry up.

But by this point, already in the VIP lounge, his passport won't be inspected again. All he has to do is board the plane. That's what his friend said in the car, an older man with a Mercedes 190 who gave him a ride to Kinshasa's N'djili International Airport. This settles Massamba somewhat. The friend, a government worker with all kinds of connections, arranged everything. Counterfeit passport, plane tickets. And he managed to convince an acquaintance who was high up at the airport to get Massamba into the VIP lounge.

The day is bright and clear. Looking out of the car window on the way to the airport, the sky seemed to shimmer with tiny silver flames. Massamba will never forget the dazzling light of that day – 30 September 2008 – and how it stands in stark contrast to the gloom in his heart.

At long last there is an announcement for his flight to Ethiopia. He stands. Hurry, the refrain keeps on in his mind, hurry. He continues past the people he left the lounge with, back towards economy, he sits, fastens his seat belt. Before long he hears over the PA that the doors have been closed. The plane eases into motion.

'That was the moment. The weight that had been on my shoulders finally disappeared. My whole body felt lighter.' Massamba tells me this now, thinking back to that day. He exhales long and slow.

The plane takes off. Finally, the danger is behind him. Relief floods his whole body, and all he wants is to submerge himself in it. What happens next he can worry about later.

It is the first time Massamba has ever been on a plane, and it is bearing him to a place completely unknown to him. The ticket his friend arranged will take him to Addis Ababa, then to Bangkok, where he will change planes and take one more flight to Narita International Airport.

Japan? For Massamba, who has spent his entire life in the Democratic Republic of Congo (DR Congo), it is an utterly unfamiliar land.

.　　　.　　　.

And Japan, in turn, knows little about the faraway DR Congo, the world's eleventh largest country, boasting rich reserves of cobalt, copper and diamonds. If people know enough about the DR Congo to form an impression, it tends to be a negative one.

The 2016 Summer Olympics in Rio de Janeiro was notable for including a group of refugee athletes. Two of them, who were living in Rio, competed in judo, Popole Misenga and Yolande Bukasa Mabika, and their involvement received a lot of attention in Japan, the birthplace of judo. Their birthplace, meanwhile, was the DR Congo. Both athletes had been embroiled in civil war and had to flee when they were young, growing up separated from their families.

Present-day DR Congo won its independence from Belgium in 1960, known as the Year of Africa (the same year another country to the west with almost the same name declared independence from France, and to distinguish between the two the DR Congo is often called Congo-Kinshasa, after its capital). The military leader Joseph-Désiré Mobutu (Mobutu Sese Seko as of 1972) staged coups in 1960 and 1965, declaring himself president in 1965 and maintaining an authoritarian regime for more than thirty years. In 1971, he renamed the nation the Republic of Zaire. Mobutu orchestrated a radical transformation of the government and seized any companies financed by foreign investment. At the same time he turned a blind eye to rampant corruption at the highest levels of authority. Mobutu's power grew steadily weaker until rebel forces led by Laurent-Désiré Kabila triggered a civil war in 1996 (the First Congo War). Mobutu died in 1997. The same year, the new president Kabila gave the country its current name, the DR Congo. But there was resistance to Kabila's equally oppressive rule, with

217

frequent outbreaks of violent conflict between 1998 and 2002 (the Second Congo War).

On top of these two wars, there was massive unrest in the east of the DR Congo through the second half of the 1990s. During a ten-year period beginning in 1998, some 5.4 million people lost their lives to violence, disease and famine.

President Kabila was assassinated in 2001 and his son Joseph Kabila became the next president. He signed a peace agreement with the anti-government forces, then in December 2005 enacted a popular referendum to approve a constitution that would enable the country to hold presidential and parliamentary elections. That referendum would prove to be a critical turning point in Massamba's life.

Massamba Mangala was born in 1975 and raised in Mbanza-Ngungu, a city in the western Bas-Congo (Kongo Central since 2015) province, not far from the Atlantic. The whole family – all told, twelve brothers and sisters – moved there when his father got a job in a railway storehouse. The houses had no electricity, but people passed their days peacefully. Mbanza-Ngungu, like many cities in Congo, was a multilingual space, where you could hear people speaking Kikongo, Lingala, Tshiluba and the French that was taught in school. Massamba could switch fluidly between Kikongo, Lingala and French.

There was a military base in Mbanza-Ngungu with a vast training ground where Massamba and his friends would go to play football. When he was in primary school, he had a teacher who stressed the importance of hard work and brought the students to the forest outside the city to teach them how to cut down trees for lumber and gather grasses for thatching their roofs. Massamba remembers those times fondly.

In 1990, when he was fifteen, he went to Kinshasa to study at the Institut Rivière. Leaving his parents' home, he stayed in a small house with an uncle in the Selembao district in the south of Kinshasa. The area was hilly and heavy rains often brought mudslides that would halt all traffic.

The Institut Rivière was a six-year state school for students aged thirteen to eighteen. Massamba enrolled at fifteen, putting him two academic years behind, and he didn't graduate until he was twenty-one. He had top marks in mathematics and often helped his classmates understand the problem sets. Seeing this, one teacher invited him to consider staying on after graduation and becoming a maths instructor.

'I liked teaching. So I was happy to accept,' says Massamba. 'I was certain that I was meant to be a teacher. When I'm teaching, I feel at ease.'

It's true that Massamba always lays out what he wants to say in a logical and orderly fashion. The way a natural scientist might speak.

Before long, Massamba began teaching geography in addition to maths. By that time, the Congo was in upheaval. In 1997, Laurent Kabila led his rebel army into Kinshasa and Mobutu died in Morocco. But according to Massamba, though there was fierce fighting all around, Kinshasa itself was relatively calm and he never felt he was in any particular danger. He and a girlfriend had three children, but he took his children and left her, marrying another woman. Then he decided to move his family to his father's home town in Songololo, back in his own home province of Bas-Congo. That was in 2002.

In his new home, Massamba took a job teaching maths and geography at a local school, at the same time becoming deeply involved with the Bundu dia Kongo movement (often known simply as BDK). BDK is a political, cultural and religious organisation that originated in Bas-Congo in 1969. Historically, a tribe of people known as the Congo lived along the Atlantic coast in an area reaching from the southern part of the Republic of Congo, across Bas-Congo, to Luanda in the north of Angola. BDK aimed to preserve and promote the rights and standing of the Congo people. Politically speaking, it was organised towards winning greater self-governance in the region.

When I ask him if that isn't a movement based on radical racial politics, Massamba quietly asks me a question of his own. 'Don't you think it's perfectly natural to fight for your culture and traditions?'

Massamba's face is placid and his voice remains soft and measured. His role in BDK was to share the movement's ideas and goals, to enlighten the masses. He tells me he would get so fired up in his oratory that he developed a reputation. 'Everyone told me that once I started talking I'd never stop,' he said. It's impossible for me to picture this quiet man sitting before me as such an energetic activist. How could such a peaceful person be condemned to die?

'So what exactly happened?' I ask, and Massamba tells me the chain of events that brought him to faraway Japan – his voice quiet as usual, so that I need to lean forward over the table to catch all of it.

In December 2005 there was a citizen referendum to ratify the new constitution. BDK was distancing itself from the Kabila regime and opposed the constitution, so it called upon supporters to boycott the referendum. This was in no way illegal. BDK members filled the streets of Songololo. That's when something happened that no one foresaw: the police opened fire on the demonstrators. People fled in panic. The protest was silenced with force.

The next day, the police came to Massamba's home. He was arrested, taken to prison and put in a holding cell with nearly twenty other BDK members. Eight days later he was released. While he was in custody, the guards jeered and said filthy things, but there was no physical violence. Thinking back now, he says at that stage he still didn't feel afraid.

In February 2007, Bas-Congo held regional elections. BDK staged a large-scale demonstration, charging that the government had tampered with the results. There was a violent clash between the demonstrators, who were mainly BDK supporters, and the police and military-administered peacekeeping authorities. Officers and soldiers opened fire, turning the scene into a bloody slaughter. A UN investigation declared that at least one hundred people had been killed.

After that, the central government in Kinshasa systematically ousted Bas-Congo people from the provincial government, filling any important administrative or police positions with their cronies. In the face of that, BDK staged another large protest in February 2008. The authorities responded by moving to wipe out BDK.

'They mobilised the military and began killing citizens,' Massamba tells me.

According to the international NGO Human Rights Watch, more than two hundred people affiliated with BDK were murdered and BDK gathering sites were demolished. In March of that year, the government outlawed BDK.

Now there was no way Massamba could ignore the danger to his life. He immediately sent his wife and three children to

221

go and stay with her family, across the border in Angola, and he hid in the home of an acquaintance who lived in a village twenty miles from Songololo. His acquaintance kept Massamba informed of what was happening in town; specifically, that the police were going to the homes of BDK members one by one and taking them away.

'Many of my friends are still in prison. And there are many who were taken out of prison and never heard from again,' Massamba says. Then he looks me in the eye. 'You can guess what happened to them.'

And then came the news that Massamba had feared: a subpoena had been delivered to his home. He knew that this time he wouldn't get off as easily as he had done before. It was highly likely this would mean the end of his life.

Here in Japan, where despite our problems we're protected by the rule of law, it may be difficult to grasp just how precarious Massamba's situation was. It seems inconceivable that someone who broke no laws could be arrested, tortured and killed. Sadly, there are more than a few countries in the world where this sort of thing can happen all too easily, and the DR Congo is one of them. Massamba had good reason to fear for his life.

The Human Rights Watch report claimed that the authorities summarily executed over five hundred people in Kinshasa and Bas-Congo. Nearly one thousand more were unlawfully arrested and tortured. Somehow Massamba, a dedicated BDK partisan, was able to make it out alive.

Massamba left Bas-Congo for Kinshasa, hiding out in the west of the city, in the home of a friend from his student days. He thought if he laid low for a while things might calm down and he could return to Bas-Congo.

But a phone call from a friend working at the public safety bureau in Bas-Congo made it clear that there was no going back. 'I saw it. Your name is on the police wanted list.'

The fear of death sent a shiver through Massamba. That's when he made up his mind. He had to leave the country.

'And you didn't want to go somewhere nearby, like the Republic of the Congo or Angola?' Massamba smiles sadly at my naive question and shakes his head.

'The governments are all working together. I would be sent back right away. I know people that happened to.'

'What about your family? Didn't you want to take them with you?'

Massamba sighs.

'If I could have I would have. But it wasn't possible.'

Where could he run to? He had a friend in government who had been helping him since his arrival in Kinshasa, and when Massamba asked him this, the answer was immediate.

'Go to the Japanese embassy.'

'Japan?'

'It's always empty over there. You should be able to get a visa no problem.'

Unsure what to expect, Massamba went to the Japanese embassy in Kinshasa at 10 a.m. on 16 August 2008. It was just as his friend had said. Not a single person waiting in line at the inquiries desk. Only Massamba. And the Japanese man at the desk, who might very well have been the consul, checked the application documents himself. Massamba was surprised when the man said that he should be able to issue a visa by the end of the day. Two days later, Massamba returned. He handed over his passport and received it back almost immediately, the visa affixed inside. Still not quite believing it, Massamba stared at the passport that his friend had procured for him. There was a name in Swahili, his name, but not his name at all.

Massamba planned to apply for asylum as a refugee as soon as he arrived in Japan. The Refugee Convention defines a refugee as a person who 'owing to a well-founded fear of being persecuted for reasons of race, religion, nationality, membership of a particular social group or political opinion, is outside the country of his nationality.' As a member of BDK, a group persecuted by the government of the DR Congo, Massamba faced a very real threat of persecution if he remained in his country, and was therefore, in no uncertain terms, a refugee.

There cannot be many refugees who, like Massamba, fled to an unknown country completely on their own. Take the Syrian refugees pouring into Europe since 2015. The majority of them went through brokers, crossing borders in groups and sailing the Mediterranean Sea. At the very least they were with other refugees who spoke the same language and could talk about where they planned to go, how they intended to live, their hopes and fears. For Massamba, there was no one.

On the flight from Suvarnabhumi International Airport in Thailand to Narita, he met a man from Cameroon who was working for a Japanese company. But when Massamba explained his situation and asked if the man happened to know anyone in Japan from the DR Congo, anyone who might help him, the man's attitude changed slightly. As if he'd become suspicious of Massamba, as if he wanted to keep his distance. And when they landed at Narita and disembarked, the man walked off quickly, as if hoping Massamba wouldn't try to talk to him. Before long Massamba lost track of the man in the throng of people spread out before the immigration booths. Then in the arrivals hall, Massamba spotted him again, and called out hopefully. The moment their eyes met the man flashed a look of surprise and annoyance. Massamba realised forlornly that the man wished to have nothing to do with him, even though Massamba wasn't trying to cause him any trouble.

'Sorry, I'm in a hurry,' the man said curtly, and disappeared onto a bus.

Not knowing what else he could do, Massamba found a taxi and got in. He showed the driver his hotel's address. First he'd go to the hotel and rest. After a good night's sleep, he planned to find the UN regional office. He was sure that the UNHCR would have an office in Japan.

The taxi brought him to the Mitsui Garden Hotel in Ginza. Massamba was taken aback at the fare: 280 dollars. He only had 3,000, scraped together by his brothers and sisters and cousins before he left. When he checked in to the hotel and asked the price, he found it was 180 dollars per night. At that rate he'd burn through his money in no time.

Massamba checked out first thing the next morning. He stepped out of the hotel and started walking. Strangely, he couldn't seem to get anywhere.

'I didn't know where I was going, and somehow I kept ending up back at the hotel.'

Apparently noticing this perplexed-looking foreigner, a young Japanese man addressed him in English. But Massamba barely spoke English. He could not get his message across. In the end he pulled a piece of paper from his bag and wrote on it 'UNHCR'. The young man seemed to understand and looked up the address on his phone, then wrote it down on the piece of paper. He led Massamba to a taxi stand and told the driver where to go. He watched Massamba get in and walked off.

Meeting the kind young man bolstered Massamba's spirits somewhat. It made him feel that if he applied for refugee status at UNHCR's Japan office, everything would be all right.

After a short drive through urban Tokyo the taxi came to a stop. Across the street was a building with various agencies and offices related to the UN. Then there was a bit of a problem: when Massamba tried to pay the fare, the driver looked flustered and waved his hand repeatedly, saying 'No, no,' in English.

The driver seemed to be saying that he wouldn't accept payment in US dollars, and managed to communicate that he would take Massamba to a bank to change his money. Massamba had no choice but to agree. The taxi pulled off, leaving behind the UNHCR office that he had tried so hard to reach.

The taxi driver parked his cab and accompanied Massamba into the bank, out of concern or perhaps a lack of trust. They finished changing the money and went back outside. Just then Massamba spotted a man who he was sure was African. He waved at the man automatically. 'Because he was from Africa like me.'

The man stopped and said something to Massamba in fluent English. He wore a T-shirt and jeans, and didn't stand as tall as Massamba, but he was solidly built. He said he was from Ghana. Massamba's English wasn't good enough to understand anything beyond that. 'Where are you going?' asked the man. But Massamba couldn't explain himself in English. Instead he took out the piece of paper that he and the young Japanese man had written on before, and wrote the English word 'refugee'. That seemed to make everything click for the Ghanaian. Just a moment, the man said, and he took out his phone and dialled somewhere. As he was talking he jotted down a number on the paper. Then he hung up and explained the situation to

Massamba. 'I just spoke to my friend. He said if you are applying for refugee status, you should go here instead.' He pointed
to what he had scribbled on the paper. 'It's a small organisation
for processing refugee asylum applications in Japan. If you go
to the UN they'll send you here, so you might as well go here
first. But I don't have the address.'

Then the Ghanaian started talking to the taxi driver in
Japanese. 'Don't worry, I'll take it from here.' He had Massamba
pay the cab fare and then beckoned him. 'Come with me.'

The Ghanaian led Massamba to a little square building
fronting the street – Massamba hadn't yet started studying
Japanese and didn't know that these buildings were called
'police boxes' – where there were two officers.

'Were you worried when you saw the police?' I ask, aware
of how much trouble Massamba had had with the authorities
in Bas-Congo. But as soon as I heard his answer I regretted
asking such a stupid question.

'Why should I be?' he smiled. 'I hadn't done anything
wrong! I never broke a single law, neither in the Congo nor in
Japan. I came to Japan seeking asylum as a refugee. If anything
I would expect the police to help me.'

When one of the officers spoke to the Ghanaian, the man
handed over the piece of paper with the phone number. The
officer promptly made a call. He seemed to be asking for the
address, which he wrote down, then he returned the piece of
paper to the Ghanaian.

They left the police box and the Ghanaian hailed a taxi and
had Massamba get in. He spoke to the driver in Japanese and
showed him the address. The driver appeared to understand.

At their parting the Ghanaian said: 'Good luck.'

.   .   .

And so, on the sixth floor of an old building in the Yotsuya neighbourhood, Massamba came to the office of the Japan Association for Refugees, a non-profit civic organisation established in 1999 that functioned as the primary advocate for refugees in Japan.

Not for a moment did he imagine the seven-year ordeal that awaited him.

At the office, Massamba received advice on how best to fill out the confusing refugee asylum application forms and got a recommendation for an inexpensive hotel. He spent a week getting his forms in order and then headed for the Immigration Bureau in Shinagawa.

But he ended up taking the wrong exit from the massive Shinagawa Station and got completely lost. He watched the people streaming by in all directions, hoping to find someone like the kind young Japanese man or the Ghanaian, but eventually gave up and returned to his hotel. The next time he tried he managed to find the bureau. But none of the doors to the building would open. This didn't make sense at first, since it wasn't a weekend. It turned out to be a national holiday.

On his third attempt he finally managed to submit his application forms. That was 14 October 2008. Massamba explained the circumstances of his flight from his country, including the reason why the name on his passport differed from his actual name. The official responded in a perfunctory tone: 'Entering the country with a counterfeit passport is a violation of Japanese law.' This blindsided Massamba.

At this point he was still unaware of how unwelcoming Japan as a country is towards refugees. Of 7,568 applicants for asylum in 2015, the largest number in Japanese history, only twenty-seven were granted refugee status. In 2008, the year Massamba applied, there were 1,599 applications in total, with only fifty-seven approved, which was the highest number of successful applications in the ten-year period since 2006. While the number of applications has risen steadily since 2010, the percentage of those accepted remains staggeringly low. In 2010, for instance, only 1.9 per cent of applicants were successful.

So Massamba succeeded in submitting his forms, but that was no guarantee his case would be processed any time soon. And since he entered Japan with someone else's name on his passport, that is, with a counterfeit passport, he was technically an illegal alien, which strictly limited his movements. Although the Shinagawa Immigration Bureau granted him a temporary residence permit, he needed to have it renewed every six months, and he was not allowed to leave the Tokyo region until a final verdict was reached on his case. If he had to leave the area he needed to apply for special permission at the Immigration Bureau. And while his application was being processed he was prohibited from working.

How was he supposed to survive if he didn't work? He was eligible for a public assistance stipend from the Ministry of Foreign Affairs, just under 90,000 yen per month (roughly eight hundred dollars) to spend on housing and daily needs. But without legal resident status, if he were to get sick, for example, he would have to pay for medical care out of his own pocket.

Massamba was summoned to the Shinagawa Immigration Bureau for an interview in December 2009. That's more than a whole year after he submitted his application.

I express surprise at that, but Massamba just answers quietly, 'I know people who have waited longer. I was one of the luckier ones.'

But Massamba left the interview feeling anxious. Apparently the back and forth with the official had been less than smooth. He wasn't sure if the Japanese woman acting as French interpreter was properly getting his words across. He was asked repeatedly about things he had already explained: the conversation kept going around in circles. His case was decided in March 2010. His fears were justified: he was turned down.

Massamba immediately filed for an appeal, so that his case could be considered again. The next interview did not take place until 16 November 2012, two years and eight months after he filed for appeal. By that time he had the sense that something was profoundly wrong with the refugee asylum application process in Japan. What's more, the interpreter was the same woman from last time. The proceedings were just as halting as they had been in his first interview, causing the normally affable Massamba to become furious.

Nearly three months later, on 7 February 2013, a decision was reached. By that point Massamba had been in Japan for five years.

His appeal was rejected. It seemed he was unable to gain refugee status, no matter what he did.

But that wasn't the worst of it. At the same time as being notified that his appeal was being denied, he was informed that, due to his having entered Japan with a counterfeit passport and his status being that of an illegal resident, he would be deported back to his home country. He was to be detained that very day at the Shinagawa Immigration Bureau.

The luckiest thing to happen to Massamba since his arrival in Japan – and he stresses this to me over and over again in the course of our conversation – was that, shortly after first submitting his application for refugee status, he became acquainted with members of the Kalabaw Society, a civil group based in Yokohama that helps foreigners living in Japan with work and life difficulties.

At the end of 2008, Massamba moved into the Choseikan ('Long-life House'), a boarding house in the Kotobukicho neighbourhood of the Naka ward in Yokohama. The Japanese school he had been attending was rather far away from his new lodgings, and the train fare to get there started to add up. He began looking for somewhere closer by to study Japanese. When he asked the YMCA worker who had directed him to the Choseikan, that person told him about the Japanese course offered by the Kalabaw Society. It was close enough for him to walk to from his boarding house.

'Where are you from? Why did you come to Japan? The people of the Kalabaw Society were very interested to learn about me, and very kind,' Massamba recalls. 'But I don't speak English, and they didn't speak French. It was difficult to communicate.'

But when Kalabaw Society members were participating in a summer festival in the working-class neighbourhood of Kotobukicho, they happened to meet Shintaro Namioka, an associate professor in the international studies department at Meiji Gakuin University. Namioka's research was on Islamic practice among immigrant populations in Europe. He had spent considerable time studying and researching in France and was fluent in French. Meeting Namioka was an unexpected stroke of good fortune, both for Massamba and for the people of the Kalabaw Society, who were hoping to learn more about their new member. They asked Namioka to translate for them, to which he happily agreed. They set a meeting. Talking to Namioka, Massamba finally felt like someone was actually understanding him. And through Namioka, the rest of the Kalabaw Society finally understood Massamba's situation. They resolved to do everything they could to help him.

Namioka invited Massamba to international studies lectures and international peace workshops at his university, deepening their relationship. He also arranged for his students to study French with Massamba, beginning in February 2010 and hosted by the Kalabaw Society. For Massamba, who felt he was born to be a teacher, this was a source of great joy.

Massamba's first application for refugee asylum was decided in March 2010. When he went to hear the verdict at the Shinagawa Immigration Bureau, Namioka and the Kalabaw Society members went with him. Massamba was, of course, dejected at being turned down, but the Kalabaw Society encouraged him. 'We'll get you legal help,' they said. That was how the lawyer Hajime Kanbara entered the circle of people helping Massamba.

Even when Massamba's appeal was denied and he was held at the Shinagawa Immigration Bureau, the Kalabaw Society never wavered in their support.

But Massamba was in custody, and would soon be deported back to the DR Congo! He was a refugee, who had come to Japan in fear for his life. They were not about to let him be sent back. The Kalabaw Society organised a 'Help Massamba' campaign, attracting backing from the Refugee Empowerment Network and the Kanazawa Human Rights Centre, among other groups, as well as from Namioka, his students, and individuals including foreign residents of Japan. Massamba's circle of support grew wider. It was plain to see that Massamba had earned the love and trust of all kinds of people since his arrival in Japan.

On 26 April 2013, while Massamba was still being detained, the lawyer Kanbara filed a suit with the Japanese government demanding that Massamba's refugee status be approved. The first public hearing in the Tokyo district court took place on 19 July. Massamba was not permitted to attend.

Then on 16 August he was released from custody and provisionally cleared of charges (which required Kanbara to serve as his guarantor and the 'Help Massamba' group to post bail). That meant he had been held by the government for six months – or, to be as precise as Massamba prefers to be, six months and ten days. The whole time he had regular visitors from the 'Help Massamba' crowd, which surprised the guards at the detention centre. They wanted to know: 'Who is this guy, anyway?'

The case ended up spanning thirteen public hearings in the Tokyo district court. The first session was in July 2013 and the last was two years later, in August 2015.

'How did you make ends meet during all that time?' I ask.

I was curious, because even though he was granted provisional clemency, the public assistance funds he had relied on previously were cut off. He was only permitted to be in the country because he was involved in an active legal case, so naturally he was forbidden from working.

'My "Help Massamba" friends. They never let me down, never. They helped out with money and they brought me rice and other foods,' he reminisces earnestly.

I imagine that having to live off the generosity of others would engender a deep sense of indebtedness, perhaps even powerlessness.

233

'It must have been rough on you, waiting through that long trial.'

'Of course. There was nothing I could do. I felt a great darkness. I tried not to let it show on the outside, but there was a constant ache in my heart. It was terrible. Once I was detained I asked myself over and over – I did not break any laws, I was honest about everything, I never told a single lie, so why is all of this happening to me?' Massamba's voice is soft.

'Did you ever feel like giving up?'

'Almost. But whenever I talked to the people from the Kalabaw Society I felt a bit better. I felt brave. They gave me strength and hope.'

On 28 August 2015, the Tokyo district court reached its final verdict: Massamba's original request would be granted and all charges against him dropped. He was officially granted refugee status. The court judged that Massamba was telling the truth.

The government had two weeks to challenge the court's decision. But the challenge never came. This meant that the state acknowledged the Immigration Bureau and the Ministry of Justice had not initially handled Massamba's case properly.

The case was closed. On 26 October 2015, Massamba went to the Shinagawa Immigration Bureau, filled out the proper paperwork and received a residency card. He had finally been granted asylum.

The Japan Association for Refugees arranged for me to meet Massamba and hear his story. We met on a Sunday in mid-July 2016, at a café in Oshiage, under the Tokyo Skytree. He lives in this area now, in a small apartment not far from the Skytree. Because he now has permanent resident status he is registered for national health insurance. He also studies Japanese five days a week through a course provided by the Refugee Assistance Headquarters, a division of the Ministry of Foreign Affairs. He shows me his Japanese study notebook. It's full of small, neatly-penned writing practice, hiragana and katakana and simple kanji characters. The fact that he's carrying his notebook with him on a Sunday when his class doesn't meet gives me a sense of his diligence. His next challenge is to look for work. I doubt it will be easy. 'I was a teacher. I can speak French, so maybe I can find a job teaching French,' he says calmly. His soft voice is nearly lost in the conversation and laughter of the other café patrons. 'I'd love to get better at Japanese and work as an interpreter. I could be a bridge between Japan and French-speaking Africa. Africa needs Japan.'

This coming from a man who had to wait seven years for his refugee status to be approved. But in the course of our conversation, he never once expresses any anger or resentment towards the country that was so stubborn in granting him aid. 'There are many people who waited much longer than I did,' Massamba says. He never exaggerates his case, maintaining an objective perspective.

I ask about the time he spent detained at the Shinagawa Immigration Bureau. 'Did the guards treat you properly? Did anything bad happen to you?'

When I ask that, Massamba gives me an answer that exemplifies his forthright integrity.

'Anything bad? No, not at all. There was no violence at all. If the detainees broke the rules, the guards got annoyed or angry, but that's perfectly understandable. We are in Japan, so we must obey Japanese law. No one is above the law.'

He respects the rule of law, and he knows all too well that when it doesn't function properly it leads to tragedy. The laws of his own country failed to protect him, so he had to leave the Democratic Republic of Congo behind. And the laws of Japan formed a high, solid wall that tried to keep him out. For Massamba, who believes that no one is above the law, the only way forward was to rely on the help of the Kalabaw Society to make it over that ill-conceived wall. In the end it took him seven years.

We leave the café and walk together. The Skytree looms above us.

'Have you ever been to the top?' I ask.

A smile flickers on Massamba's face and he shakes his head gently. 'No, never.'

'I guess sometimes we overlook the things that are right in front of us.'

Massamba and I part ways and I head for Oshiage Station. Maybe because it's Sunday, there are throngs of people here to see Tokyo's newest attraction. I see tourists from all over the world.

Tourists?

If I didn't know Massamba's story and I saw him standing there, I'm sure I would assume he was a tourist too. But there are people like Massamba, refugees, all around us. We just don't think about it.

FRAGMENTS FROM
THE LIFE OF THE
SPECTACULAR VICTIM

ECE TEMELKURAN

One of Turkey's best known authors and political commentators, ECE TEMELKURAN was born in Izmir, Turkey, in 1973, and has published twelve books, including the 2013 novel *The Women Who Blow on Knots*, published in English by Parthian Books and translated into twenty-two languages. Her investigative reporting on controversial topics has been honoured with numerous awards, including the German government's Journalist of the Year Award (1996) and the Pen for Peace (2001). Her latest book, *The Insane and the Melancholy* (2016), published in English by Zen Books, has been highly praised by critics.

I was supposed to be writing about a refugee in Istanbul. Then she disappeared. Most of them do disappear now and again. Then I had to disappear myself. So I am now the subject of this text, although I am not a refugee but in self-imposed exile, or a seemingly self-imposed exile. Does the terminology matter if you feel the constant heartache of that Syrian woman, talking to a journalist on the Turkish coast upon her arrival last summer, saying, 'I wish I was dead so my pride would not be broken like this'?

Pride is the one basic need an exile or refugee must supply for themselves. There's no refugee centre or NGO that can help you with that. You find these things out while learning that living is far more complicated than not dying.

Is there an honourable way of dealing with the reality of being obliged to leave your home? Or is the question of pride a luxury available only to those able to whine eloquently about it? What happens to the exiles who do not have the fancy words that I do? They become numbers. Numbers are crossing the Mediterranean right now. And by the way, some numbers are drowning in the sea. Look, there they are! Other numbers are making it to shore. Surviving numbers are even applying for 'papers'. Now these numbers have to live. They have to recover their names.

There is a page on the UNHCR web page called 'Refugees Who Have Made a Difference'. There are only twenty profiles listed. So the thousands of others who drowned in the ocean remain nameless numbers, even those who survived the journey remain anonymous. Those who succeed in crossing the Mediterranean are obliged to go on another difficult journey to become a person.

I'm amazed people do not obsess about the possibility of coming across a dead body on a Mediterranean beach while swimming on their summer holidays, of touching those refugees who could not 'make a difference'.

I am not a number. I have my name printed on books in several languages. I have people asking me: 'What title do you prefer in front of your name? Author or author and journalist?' But even I've become a know-it-off-by-heart paragraph now: 'who lost her job due to the political oppression and had to leave Turkey' etc… This little paragraph that I drag along behind me supposedly tells the most important thing about me, with the rest of me supplied on demand to keener enthusiasts.

Times of oppression create the spectacular oppressor and the spectacular victim. I am now supposed to fill the shoes of this person called 'the victim'. It is a full-time job, a non-stop act. Like a refugee waiting for a piece of bread with a stupid ticket in her hands, I should be ready to perform my victimhood whenever the act is called to the intellectual stage. I am now obliged to tell a story, but only the one particular story, the stupid story of my suffering that I hold like a ticket for my passage to the civilised world. I am so ill-suited to the role that at one point, at a Frontline Club book event in London, when a woman from the audience, holding her hands together with the graciousness of the Pope washing the feet of the poor, asks me, 'So what CAN WE do for you?' I answer: 'I feel like a baby panda that you're trying to adopt on a website!'

Nobody laughs.

The victim should be the victim but nothing else. Otherwise it becomes confusing for the audience. Be a number. Be a paragraph.

I remember this man from Somalia I met in a refugee camp on the Tunisian–Libyan border. It was right after Gaddafi had been killed and I was in the middle of the desert interviewing people, all from Black Africa. I was asking the same questions over and over again, 'Do you have enough water to meet your daily needs?' 'Do you have enough food to eat?' etc… And this man, smiling the most sarcastic smile I've ever seen, asked me in perfect English, 'It doesn't occur to you to ask me do I have a CV?' He was kind and mature enough to smile in a friendly way when he saw I was mortified by my own shallowness. Now I imitate the same smile to audiences when they are confused by my silly jokes, my defying the cliché of the suffering exile.

I have started doing normal things that I never actually did before. The supermarket Billa, in Zagreb, is giving away tiny stickers. If you collect enough stickers you can buy a cooking pan half price. I neither need the pan nor have the patience to collect stamps. Besides, I've never been decisive enough to pursue such goals, which actually require considerable determination. But since I'm pretending these are not extraordinary times, I do the normal thing and buy the pan with the stickers, along with my middle-class entry pass: the supermarket loyalty card. I am now not only a victim. I am now a distinguished member of the Billa shopping crowd. I keep the card in the see-through part of my wallet, covering up my Turkish driver's license. There you go, I couldn't be more normal. I now have a brand new, gentler form of identity. I am a Billa person, not an exile.

.   .   .

In fact, my new identity is as a citizen of 'Screen-Nation'. This is a supra-nation with citizens from chaotic countries who are spread about in Western countries. We look like new-generation Celtic warriors, our blue faces glued to flickering screens: computers, TVs, smartphones. Our physical beings are in different countries but our unquenchable thirst is for news from our countries of origin.

The TV is spouting news about Turkey. After hours of unblinking concentration, I finally manage to tear my face from the screen and lean out the window to smoke. From my belly down I am in the room, from my belly up I am in Zagreb. An absent-minded magician forgot to put my pieces back together after cutting me in two.

One of the things I'm learning is that arrogance is the best remedy for broken pride. If you've had your pride broken, put lots of arrogance balm on it and eventually you'll become a different person, a person you might have hated back home. I already know how easy it is to mistake wounds for organs and unwittingly use those wounds as if they were healthy body parts. This is a different version of that. I've added a body part to myself, a clumsy, prosthetic arrogance organ. I've done this by way of reaction, because arrogance is the one thing you're not allowed to have if you're an exile. You are obliged to be more humble than you have ever been before because you need help. So I am laying claim to the forbidden and being arrogant nonetheless. It makes everybody angry, even the most tender souls trying to help me. It would have made me angry too, but this is me, trying to find a way to exist unlike any other exile who has walked the planet. I say, 'I prefer not to,' and explore a Bartleby-style exile, as if there is such a thing. It makes people angry and sooner or later they tell me so. And then I'm happy because anger is the one and only emotion that can save you from being pigeonholed as a 'victim' in their eyes. And I know this is as stupid as the supermarket stickers. But I'm just trying to find my own way, as doubtless millions of others have. I claim a better defeat.

I have always been compassionately furious with Walter Benjamin. 'You fool, how could you have left it so late to leave? How could you, genius that you were, I mean how could you not have seen it coming?' I am not asking these questions any more. Because now here I am, out of the country. Not too late, on the contrary, clever enough to have maybe been too early. However, you still poison yourself. Not with the same poison that Benjamin used to commit suicide on the Spanish border, perhaps, but with a variety of different ones. Invisible poisons.

Lately Stefan Zweig, who committed suicide in 1942, has also been getting on my nerves. Why didn't you just grit your teeth and bear it for three more years and then it would all have been over? But I also know that in order to survive exile, you cut out a piece from your heart. Your heart becomes a new sculpture, one longing for the rock that it came out of. Leaving home is an irreversible act. Even when your home calls you back with loving arms, your heart, by now missing a vital piece, cannot hear the call. All it elicits is a phantom ache for the missing part, a reminder that your heart is no longer whole.

I now understand how and why a person can commit suicide. I am not the type, though. But just in case, I'm taking my Vitamin Bs. They are the new anti-depressants and available without prescription, convenient for the exile.

.   .   .

The articles I write for international media, every single one of them, appear with a picture of Erdogan, the Turkish president. All of a sudden we are a duo, like David and Goliath, or Fred Astaire and Ginger Rogers. His face is becoming the face of my country and my name inseparable from his face on newspaper pages. I find this funny somehow. Not for me, but for him. Though I am pretty sure he doesn't laugh when he reads what I write.

I am also pretty sure that, at the current rate that worldwide political insanity is sweeping the planet, all the intellectuals of the world might soon be refugees. I am listening to Meryl Streep's speech during the Hollywood Foreign Press Awards. She cries when she talks about the crudeness and cruelty of Trump. Anyone in the world capable of feeling concern is touched. Myself included. And the next day Trump's response is to say that Streep is 'overrated'. When our eyes are still wet because of Streep's speech, this vulgar response catches us off guard. The moment is symbolic of the current problem with the world. We are losing our hold of a fundamental agreement whereby if you speak to someone as a human, that human will, by default, respond in humane language. So how can we escape such a clash of values? Where do you take refuge when the entire world decides to become a bully? Who is an exile when all countries become lands of vulgarity? Soon we will all be Syrian.

A few years ago, when I likewise had to leave the country, I asked myself: 'What is a country?' My answer was that the country is a table and the abstract space which surrounds that table. The country is a moment. It is the moment when you make a spontaneous joke and your friends at the table laugh without need of further explanation, without needing the references explained.

When someone says they miss their country, they mean they miss that moment at the table, rather than the vast space that surrounds it or the eternity surrounding the moment itself.

Now my jokes are nervous because I am creeping around the endless plateau that is English. It is a sneaky language. It deceives you with the illusion of knowing it, and then at the very moment you feel confident and relax, it trips you up and jabs you with the tip of its sword, to remind you that you are a commoner who will not be accepted at Court, ever. The people seated at my table are already scattered about the world anyway. In different countries, in different lines at supermarket counters, they stand on their own wondering whether to say yes or no to the person at the counter who asks every time: 'Would you like the supermarket loyalty card?'

The people who once sat at my table were artists, musicians, writers and actors, people who are now trying to figure out the practicalities of living in a new country while deciding whether to make a spectacle out of their victimhood through art. Every one of us now has a new table in a different land. My table is a small black one that I bought at Ikea. And just as Thor Heyerdahl once built Kon-Tiki, I built it myself. Heyerdahl and his five friends were trying to prove that people from South America might once have sailed with balsa wood rafts to Polynesia to form settlements. On my Kon-Tiki, as the sole crew member, I am exploring the possibility of crossing the waters of victimhood with my pride intact. If I manage it, it will prove that people once travelled through interesting times and built settlements on the brighter side of history.

If I were a story, this period of my life might have been the best part. But I am a person. How unfortunate.

ACKNOWLEDGEMENTS

We would like to thank all the authors, translators and readers who were sympathetic to the aims of the project and made it possible for us to publish these unique texts, originally written in eight different languages. Special thanks go to Vera Michalski and the Jan Michalski Foundation for their generous support. We're also grateful to the German Foreign Office, the Heinrich Böll Foundation, the Konrad Adenauer Foundation, the Ramon Llull Institute, the German Embassy in Nigeria and the Japanese Cultural Institute in Cologne for funding, as well as to the International Cities of Refuge Network (ICORN) and the Office of the UNHCR in Berlin for communications support. Last but not least, we thank our colleagues at the Berlin International Literature Festival for their work on the management of the project and the publication of the book: Lucy Curzon, Uta Bieber, Tatjana Gridnev, Maria Röger, Tom Woweries, Andrea Shelton, Isabell Holl, Ibrahim Abdo and Bennet Hübbe.

Proceeds from this book will be donated to Refugees International, an independent organisation that advocates for lifesaving assistance and protection for displaced people and promotes solutions to displacement crises.

Ragpicker Press coordinated a pre-sale crowdfunding campaign to raise the funds to print this book. We are grateful to everyone who pre-bought a copy, without whose support this project would not have been possible.